Rapid Deployment Logistics: Lebanon, 1958

by Lieutenant Colonel Gary H. Wade, U.S. Army
October 1984

U.S. Army
Command and General
Staff College
Fort Leavenworth, KS 66027-6900

Library of Congress Cataloging in Publication Data

Wade, Gary H., 1946—
  Rapid deployment logistics—Lebanon, 1958.

  (Research survey / Combat Studies Institute, U.S. Army Command and General Staff College ; no. 3)
  "Operation Bluebat."
  "October 1984."
  Bibliography: p.
  1. Lebanon—History—Intervention, 1958. 2. United States—Supplies and stores—History—20th century. 3. Unified operations (Military science)—History—20th century. 4. Lebanon—History—Intervention, 1958—Amphibious operations. I. U.S. Army Command and General Staff College. Combat Studies Institute. II. Title. III. Series: Research survey (U.S. Army Command and General Staff College. Combat Studies Institute) ; no. 3.
  DS87.W33 1985   956.92'04   84-28543

For sale by the Superintendent of Documents, U.S. Government Printing Office, Washington, D.C. 20402

CONTENTS

Illustrations and Tables v
Acknowledgment vii
Introduction ix

Chapter
1. THE FOUNDATION 1

   Doctrine 1
   Planning 7
   Background 7
   Problems 15

2. THE DEPLOYMENT 19

   Preparation 19
   Movement 27
   Airhead 35
   Maritime Operation 37
   Result 40

3. THE FULCRUM 43

   Organization 43
   Resupply 54
   Procurement 61
   Civil Affairs 64
   Medical Support 69
   Security 72

4. CONCLUSIONS 79

   Retraction 79
   Summary 79

Appendix
   A. Plans 83
   B. Task Force 201 85
   C. Personnel and Equipment for Alpha, Bravo, and
      Charlie Forces 89
   D. On-Hand Supplies, 31 August 1958........... 93

Notes 95
Glossary 107
Bibliography 111

ILLUSTRATIONS AND TABLES

Figures

1. Organization of a Headquarters, Logistical Command A 4
2. Organization of a Headquarters, Logistical Command B 4
3. Organization of a Headquarters, Logistical Command C 5
4. Organization for Planning 12
5. Organization of Operation Grandios 22
6. Support Force 23
7. Command Organization of Operation Grandios 24
8. Organization for Operations 44
9. Organization for Operations (Final) 46
10. Land Force Organization 48
11. Organization of the 201st Logistical Command (A) 51

Maps

1. Middle East xii
2. ATF 201 Deployment Routes to Lebanon in 1958 32
3. Security Plan 73

Tables

1. Aircraft Capability 9
2. Selected Ship Capability 10
3. Types of Alerts 25
4. Summary of Claims Paid 65

ACKNOWLEDGMENT

From the onset of this study, a number of agencies and individuals provided valuable assistance to my research and writing efforts. The Combined Arms Research Library at the U.S. Army Command and General Staff College, Fort Leavenworth, Kansas, was instrumental in providing research assistance and in obtaining the necessary authority to declassify a number of documents essential to the study. Members of the Combat Studies Institute provided invaluable assistance by providing meaningful comments and by editing the numerous drafts.

I am especially indebted to the participants of the Lebanon intervention who responded to my many inquiries, particularly Maj. Gen. David W. Gray (U.S. Army, Retired), Brig. Gen Adam W. Meetze (U.S. Army, Retired), Brig. Gen. George S. Speidel (U.S. Army, Retired), Col. Dan K. Dukes (U.S. Army, Retired), and Col. Richard M. Hermann (U.S. Army, Retired). The aforementioned agencies and, more important, the people involved have made this research survey possible and are responsible to a great degree for any contribution it makes to the doctrinal community.

INTRODUCTION

The Operation

The countries of the Middle East experienced intermittent crises during the 1950s. Lebanon was no exception, as internal turmoil and outside pressures threatened its existence. This research survey, however, will not dwell on the political situation of either the entire Middle East or, specifically, Lebanon in the spring of 1958.[1] Suffice it to say, President Camille Chamoun of Lebanon made an urgent plea on 14 July 1958 to the governments of France, Great Britain, and the United States to deploy military forces to Lebanon to stabilize the situation. Received in Washington at 0600 on 14 July, this message became the first test of the Eisenhower Doctrine, which had been announced in January 1957.

Through the Middle East Resolution, or Eisenhower Doctrine, Congress authorized the United States to provide economic and military assistance to requesting nations to preserve their independence.[2] The Eisenhower Doctrine stated that the independence and integrity of these Middle East nations were vital to world peace and to the national interest of the United States. If these nations were "attacked from a country under the control of international communism then the President was authorized, upon request, to send forces to resist that attack."[3]

U.S. military analysts believed that Lebanon was threatened internally by strong and numerous rebel bands, "most of which were strengthened by Egyptian and Syrian infiltrators constituting a fifth column," and externally by the armed forces of Syria "poised in strength" along the border.[4] Given this situation, the United States intervened. President Dwight D. Eisenhower wanted "to move into the Middle East, and specifically into Lebanon, to stop the trend toward chaos."[5] Ten hours after the receipt of President Chamoun's message, the Chief of Naval Operations ordered the U.S. Sixth Fleet (Mediterranean) eastward to land Marines in Lebanon. On 14 July, the Joint Chiefs of Staff (JCS) alerted U.S. forces in Europe and the Tactical Air Command in the United States to be ready for immediate military action. The JCS also activated a Specified Command, Middle East (SPECOMME), and designated Adm. James L. Holloway, Commander in Chief, North Atlantic and Mediterranean, as the Commander in Chief, SPECOMME (CINCSPECOMME). According to a JCS memorandum, "These actions marked the beginning of operation 'Blue Bat,' the first United States airborne-amphibious operation to occur in peacetime."[6]

By 16 July, over 3,000 Marines had landed. The U.S. Army forces making up Army Task Force 201 (ATF 201) consisted of the 187th Battle Group from the 24th Infantry Division. This force began arriving in Beirut on the nineteenth, and, by the twenty-fifth, over 3,000 personnel and approximately 2,500 short tons of equipment had been brought in aboard 242 air missions.[7] Shortly thereafter, the sealift in support of the Army brought in an additional 3,650 soldiers and 45,450 measurement tons of supplies in three transports and thirteen cargo vessels.[8]

The U.S. forces landed unopposed and quickly found themselves in a role limited to showing force instead of using it. With the 31 July election of General Fuad Shehab, commander of the Lebanese army, as the new president and his subsequent inauguration on 23 September, a semblance of order returned, and U.S. forces began their departure. During the three months of American involvement, one U.S. battle death occurred, while U.S. armed forces caused no civilian casualties. The American projection of power had worked, as the political situation had at least become stabilized temporarily.

This absence of combat did not radically alter the logistical support for the force, which still had to be fed, clothed, housed, and cared for. Of course, ammunition resupply, casualty evacuation, and combat loss replacement were not important parts of the effort, but other functions, such as civil affairs, construction, and health and comfort activities, came to the fore.

Because the United States has in the past deployed military force without using it in combat (and may do so again), it is instructive to study the logistical effort behind the intervention, that is, the deployment and sustainment of this force. This research survey is concerned with the lowest level of this effort, called in some sources battlefield supply or tactical logistics. This study examines how the Army organized in 1958 to move and to support itself in the field and what process it used to do so. This research survey discusses aspects of combat service support, including such functions as resupply, transportation, procurement, civil affairs, and medical support. <u>Rapid Deployment Logistics: Lebanon, 1958</u> presents a model for planning, deploying, and sustaining a task force--a model that offers many lessons for today's Army. The absence of combat focused more attention on these aspects than would have been the case in combat operations, and the participants had the time to document their problems and recommendations. Thus, a study of this operation will be of particular benefit for the planner, logistician, and combat arms officer. This study reconstructs the logistical doctrine for a rapid deployment contingency force as it existed in 1958 and evaluates its implementation in the Lebanese crisis.

Although the Army's logistical doctrine was generally sound, rapid deployment logistical planning for contingency force operations, such as the U.S. intervention in Lebanon, was weak. Before World War II, contingency planning had focused on technical questions and tended to ignore organizational issues. Therefore, the basis of "how to accomplish tasks" or doctrine had developed in a haphazard fashion. This doctrinal development must be examined to understand the status of contingency force operations in 1958.

> GARY H. WADE
> LTC, FA
> Combat Studies Institute,
>   USACGSC

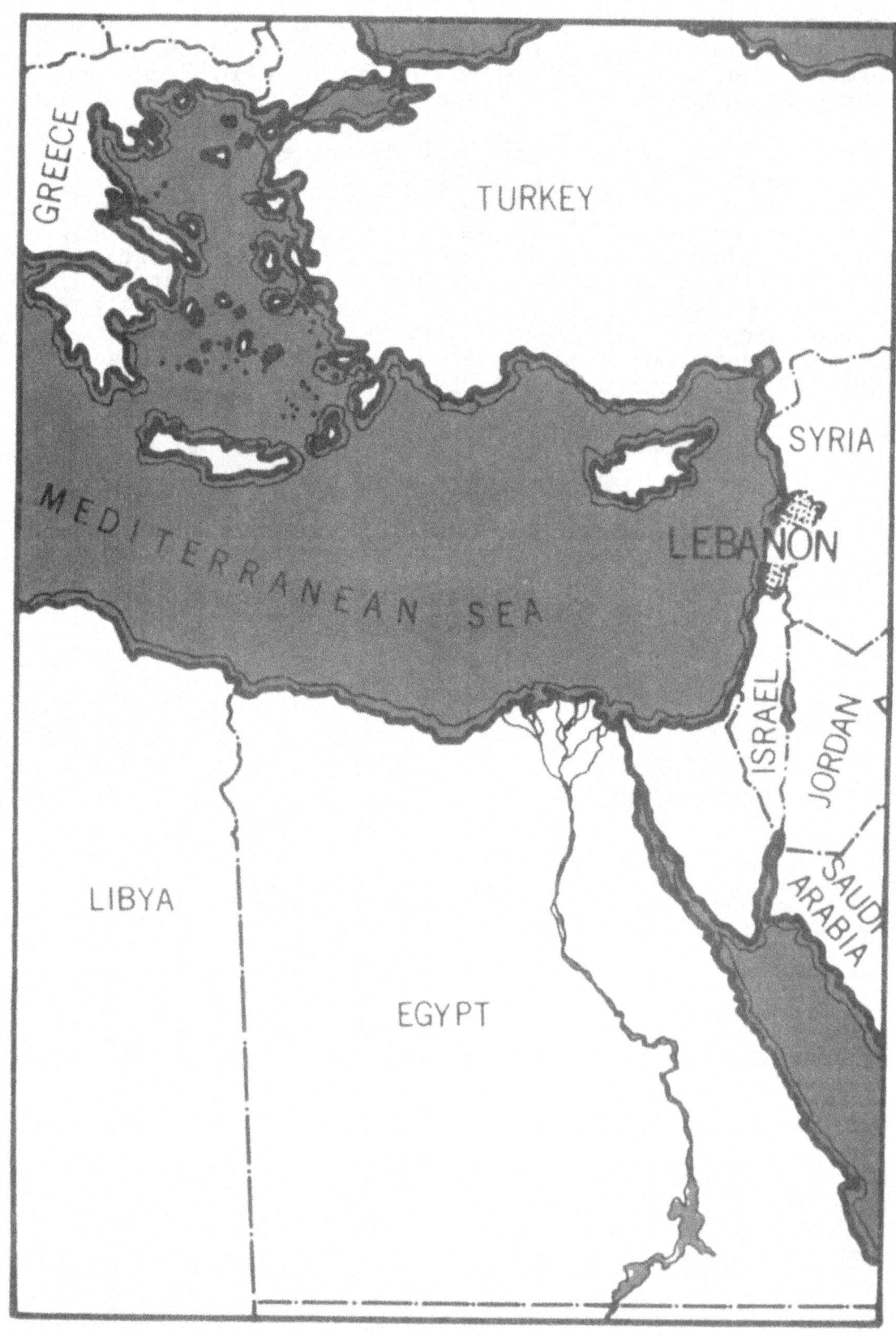

Source: Spiller, "Not War But Like War," 3.

Map 1. Middle East

CHAPTER 1

THE FOUNDATION

Doctrine

Joint Chiefs of Staff Publication Number 1 defines logistics as "the science of planning and carrying out the movement and maintenance of forces." Logistics is the procurement, maintenance, and transportation of materiel, facilities, and personnel in support of a military operation. It can mean anything from acquiring raw materials to delivering a bullet to the soldier in the field.

Gen. George C. Marshall once stated, "The requirements of logistics are seldom understood. The burdens they impose are seldom appreciated." Gen. Dwight D. Eisenhower added, "It is logistics which controls campaigns and limits many."[1] Logistics, for example, was the reason that Operation Overlord, the invasion of Normandy in World War II, and Operation Anvil, the invasion of southern France, could not occur at the same time as planned.

Today, the U.S. Army is again pondering the doctrine of how we fight and how we sustain the fight. Although moving and supporting the force has traditionally held less interest than combat, the fight cannot take place without materiel and services. Combat and combat service support should be coequal concerns on the battlefield, hence the need for studying logistical doctrine in concert with battle analysis.

Lt. Gen. Lesley J. McNair, Commanding General, Army Ground Forces (1942-44), made great innovations in the organization of ground combat units (the triangular division concept), but organizational planning for logistical units did not keep pace. The problem of logistical organization became apparent upon America's entry into that war. Before World War II, the problem of support for logistical units had largely been confined to technical studies (i.e., mathematical computation of supply rates) rather than to the organization of service units.[2]

The 1942 North African invasion demonstrated that too many officers did not yet understand elementary logistical considerations.[3] Improvisation all too often replaced a planned logistical effort. The Pacific theater also experienced numerous instances of misplaced supplies, wasted transportation, hastily organized headquarters, and shortages of critical service units.[4] For example, shortages of shipping and service troops came perilously close to costing the United States the Guadalcanal victory.[5] The resupply to overseas theaters appeared to be an ad hoc process rather than the planned, rational, and efficient system that many had thought existed.

For World War II logistics, it was essential to have a supply stockpile of so many days of materiel on hand in the forward areas. Instead of relying on a constant flow of supplies, field commanders, by and large, wanted large stocks pre-positioned before they began an operation. They were reluctant to depend on an overseas line of communication that necessitated adequate ports, large secure supply areas, and a large number of people to handle the supplies. Thus, when a communications zone (COMMZ) section was established, a headquarters would be formed. A table of distribution and allowances would be written specially for that immediate purpose and composed of people who happened to be thrown together on the job. The result was confusion and wasted effort. Furthermore, the procedure led to "empire building" because no permanent tables of organization existed.[6]

In the Continental United States (CONUS), multiple organizations and agencies were responsible for the logistical effort, but the importance of a single command was recognized by the Army Service Forces. "For the first time, there was a full recognition of the importance of logistics to the Army and the advantage of concentrating logistic operations in a single command."[7] In 1944, the Command and General Staff College studied the problem and recommended the organization of a logistical division:

> Just as the infantry division was a basic unit of combined combat arms, the logistical division would be a basic unit of combined technical and administrative services. It would have organic service and administrative units numbering approximately 26,000 men to provide communications zone support for a reinforced corps. The proposals further envisaged a logistical corps with a strength of some 67,000 men for the support of a field army.[8]

This study indicated a need for teams from each technical service to form combined units and for headquarters staffs to be formed and trained to control these teams. Teams would train together in peace for wartime employment. These general conclusions formed the basis for organizing logistical command headquarters on tables of organization and equipment (TOEs).[9] Thus, by the end of the war, World War II logistical divisions and corps had evolved.

Planning for logistics has not been one of the Army's strongpoints. Much of the planning that had occurred before World War II had been technical and not organizational in nature. Without a plan for organization and a definite chain of command, however, doctrine remains rather hazy, for either doctrine guides organization or organization sets the doctrine. In either case, plans should state how logistical units are to be controlled rather than use the ad hoc process of World War II.

In 1945, the U.S. Army dropped the logistical corps, expanded the logistical division, and tested it in 1946. After-action reports were "generally favorable." In 1949, the "logistical division" became the "logistical command," a change probably made to reserve the term "division" for combat units.[10]

Three types of logistical command TOEs existed in 1949, each one configured to support forces of different sizes. The type A logistical command consisted of a headquarters designed to command an integrated organization of technical and administrative service units ranging from 9,000 to 15,000 men who would support approximately 30,000 combat troops* (figure 1). Logistical command type B was established to command 35,000 to 60,000 personnel and would support a force of 100,000* (figure 2). A type C command consisted of between 75,000 and 150,000 men and would support more than 400,000 troops* (figure 3).[11]

The Korean War saw the first combat use of the logistical command structure.[12] The 2d Logistical Command, a type C organization, was formed in September 1950 primarily to receive, store, and forward supplies for the Eighth Army. It also forwarded requisitions to the Japan Logistical Command. After the Inchon landing, the 3d Logistical Command, a type B organization, was formed to support the X Corps. Based on their experiences, participants indicated that the concept of a table of organization logistical command appeared to be "sound in concept and realistic in proposed mission."[13] One officer noted, however, that "a smoother operation and

---

*Combat troop numbers included the assigned organic support troops of the companies, battalions, brigades, and divisions.

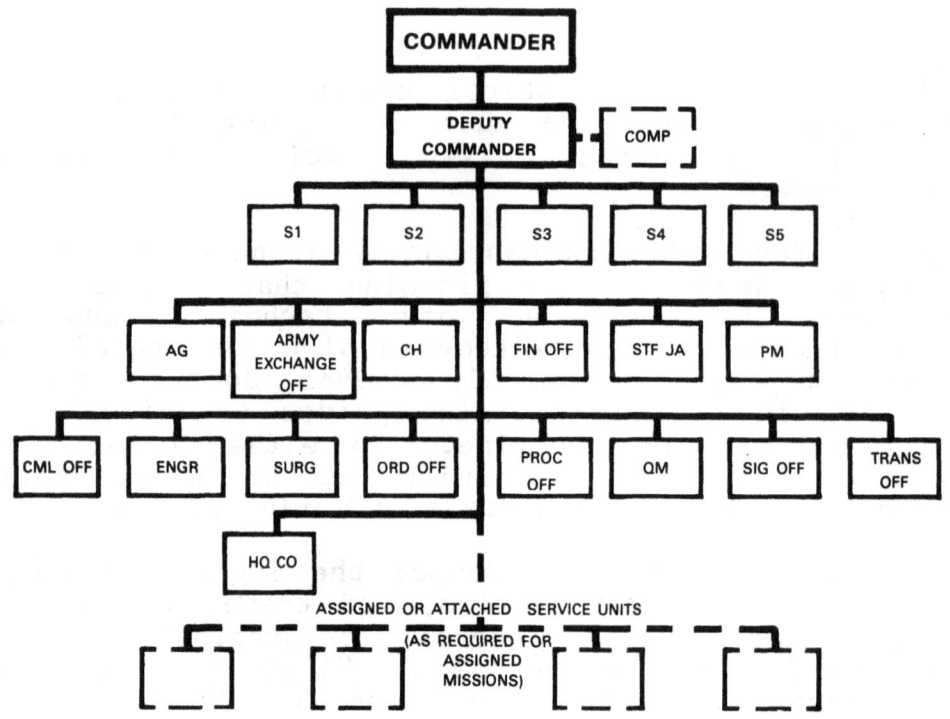

Source: CGSC, "Regular Course," 4–5.

Figure 1. Organization of a Headquarters, Logistical Command A

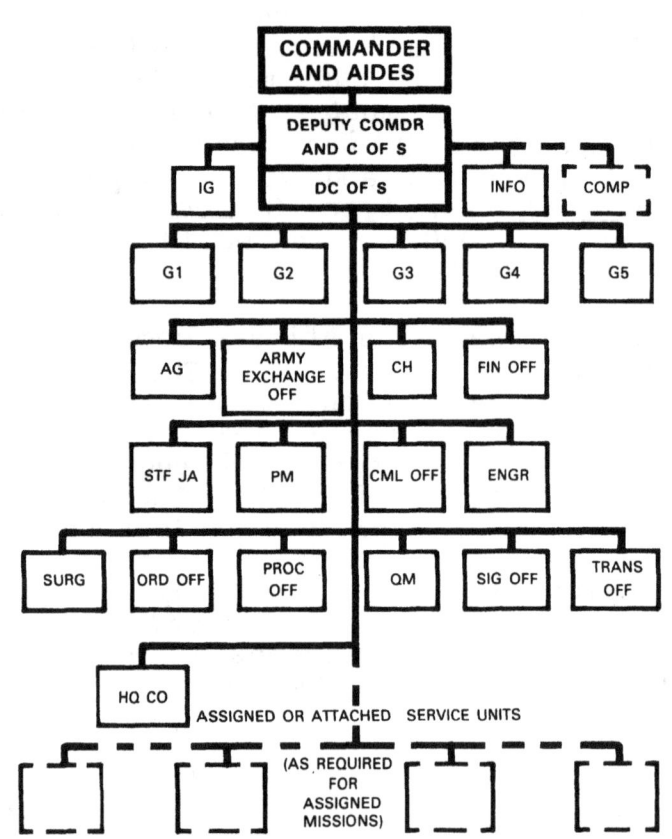

Source: CGSC, "Regular Course," 4–5.

Figure 2. Organization of a Headquarters, Logistical Command B

Source: CGSC, "Regular Course," 4—6.

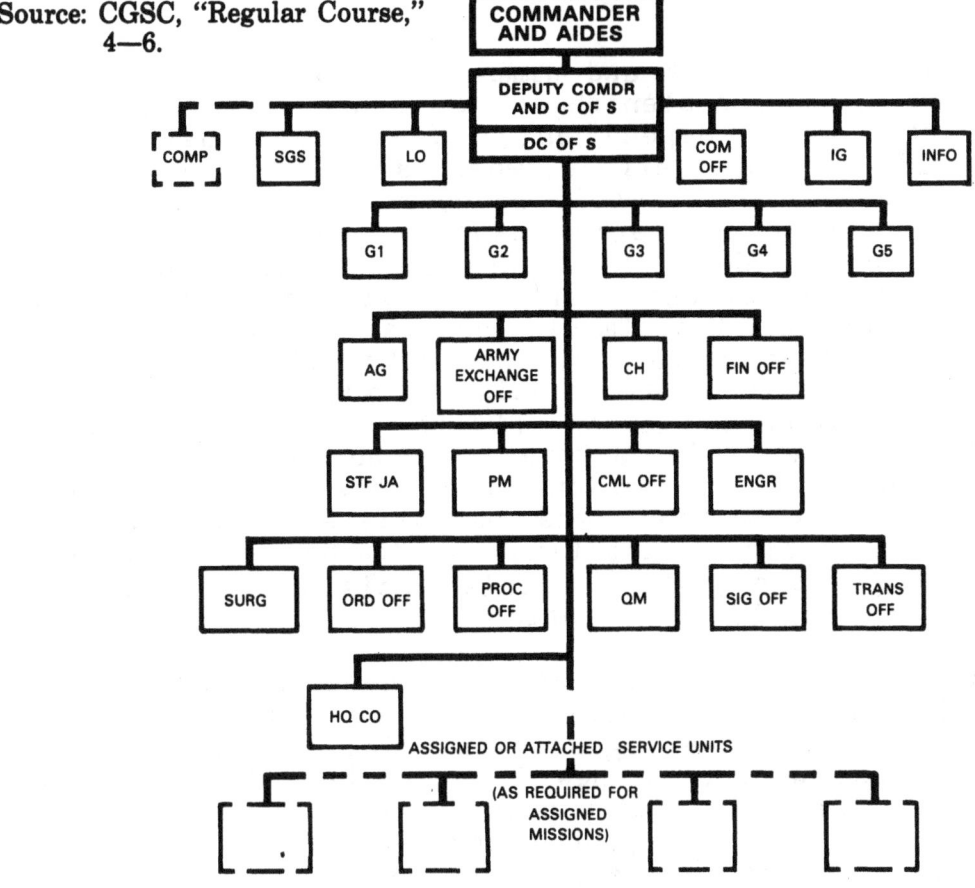

Figure 3. Organization of a Headquarters, Logistical Command C

more effective support would have resulted if organized and trained logistical commands had been available prior to the initiation of hostilities."[14] It would have been better to have had logistical commands in existence and staffed for a wartime deployment because training and teamwork are just as essential for logistical commands as they are for combat units.

Once the organization had been determined, the process for providing supplies needed to be determined. One system, a push system, automatically sent supplies to forward units based on so many days of supplies for a particular item being on-hand at all times. In a pull system, supplies were delivered forward, based on unit requisitions. A more recent development, the push-pull system, had each unit determining its needs beforehand, which were then packaged in sets and sent forward on demand of the unit. The first two of these systems were tested during World War II.

Based on World War II experience, the War Department expected three successive phases for supply operations when opening a new overseas theater. The first phase would be automatic, with calculated amounts of materiel sent to consuming units. Automatic resupply would continue until phase two was reached, generally after the beachhead was secure. Phase two would be semiautomatic:

replenishment of rations and ammunition would be based on status reports, and replenishment of other items, such as repair parts, would depend on unit requisitions. Phase three would go into effect when a theater had been stabilized, and resupply would be by requisition only. It can be argued that automatic resupply should have worked best in a stabilized theater where information would have been complete and abrupt changes in status reports less frequent. The War Department, however, determined that the beginning of an operation, when automatic resupply was the most difficult, was precisely when it was most necessary.[15] Since World War II, the Army has generally continued to use this automatic push system at the beginning of an operation and resorted to unit requisitions once a front was established, just at the time when automatic requisitions would have worked best with the least confusion.[16] This decision continued to cause problems for later operations.

This dilemma between pushing supplies forward or waiting for a unit to declare its need has been the traditional bane of the logistician. The goal of just-in-time logistics, whereby a new item reaches the user just as the old one runs out, proved as elusive as ever. Another problem with the push system was that it required many service personnel and laborers, a problem that plagued later contingency operations. For example, in the Korean War, the 2d Logistical Command eventually employed over 100,000 Koreans to make the system work.[17] This should have warned future planners regarding the need for inordinately large numbers of indigenous help to sustain the system of automatic resupply.

Still, the Korean experience seemed to validate the logistical command tailoring concept and phased resupply. In the 1950s, logistical doctrine led to the establishment of the Administrative Support System. This integrated system of personnel, units, equipment, organization, principles, procedures, and techniques was geared to provide administrative support extending from the source (the zone of the interior) to the forces in the combat area where a logistical command would be in operation. The Administrative Support System was to be designed to support tactical operations or campaigns that were to be organized as task forces tailored to a specific mission. This flexible system was also to provide the required support for a specific military operation. The origins of this system date from World War II.

So, by 1958, our logistical doctrine consisted of tailoring a logistical command to support a specific operation and then basing that support initially on automatic requisitions and phased resupply. In that same year, a preplanned logistical command supported a rapid deployment force in an operational theater. Logistical doctrine was about to confront actual planning.

Planning

The commander of the 201st Logistical Command (type A) in 1958 was Col. Adam W. Meetze. Meetze, now a retired brigadier general, commented:

> Many, many hours went into the planning for this organization and how it should operate. We utilized the philosophy that originated at Leavenworth years ago that combat commanders in an operational theatre with troops of this magnitude would have one supply unit--one individual being responsible--that he could go to for all classes of supplies, maintenance, and the support required for him to attain his combat objectives. In other words the logistics doctrine in Lebanon in 1958 was to have a logistical command tailored to specific combat units for an assigned mission. This was the first time, to the best of my knowledge, that a tailored logistical command had supported a combat force in an operational theatre.[18]

Background

In the late 1950s, the United States was moving away from a policy of massive retaliation toward more flexible military forces. To meet this requirement, Army planners reshaped divisions to meet the Pentomic structure, making divisions lighter, more mobile, and more flexible. Also, planners devised and tested new logistical concepts with a view to making drastic reductions in the supply pipelines and stockages for the support of these mobile, flexible field armies of the future.

The Army had a rapid deployment force in 1958, the Strategic Army Corps (STRAC). STRAC was to provide a flexible, mobile strike capability by using a two-division force, the 101st Airborne Division and the 4th Infantry Division. This force should have been able to be "deployed without declarations of an emergency."[19] The commanding general of the XVIII Airborne Corps was responsible for properly coordinating the necessary logistical planning. In case of a general conflict, the 1st Infantry Division and 82d Airborne Division would also join STRAC.

Deficiencies in strategic mobility became the Achilles' heel for the use of STRAC units as an instrument of national policy.[20] These deficiencies were quantitative and qualitative. The Military Air Transportation Service (MATS) had a total of 188 million ton-miles* available for all services. Army planners figured that the Army alone would need eighty million ton-miles for a general war. On 10 April 1958, Maj. Gen. Earle G. Wheeler, Office of the Deputy Chief of Staff for Operations and Plans, testified before the Department of Defense (DOD) Subcommittee on Appropriations "that the total airlift requirement stated by all the services for the first month of general war is approximately equal to the maximum Army airlift requirement for a limited war. If the general war requirement could be met, it would seem likely that the limited war requirement of the Army could be met in most situations."[21]

A limited war in the Middle East required 123 million ton-miles with a twenty-day close-in, leaving a surplus of 20 million ton-miles for additional requirements.[22] Out of a possible 188 million ton-miles, 143 million ton-miles was a sizable portion for such a limited operation. This was significant considering that much of the available ton-miles was already committed to other operational needs. Unless the President declared a national emergency, MATS probably would not be released from its priority missions of supporting the Strategic Air Command. Indeed, the question of whether the Army would even receive priority over other services in a limited operation had not been addressed.

Exacerbating the quantitative problem, the capacity for the 188 million ton-miles included over 350 commercial airline planes in the Civil Reserve Air Fleet (CRAF) earmarked for supporting military operations in an emergency. CRAF would have been useful for troop lift, but not for more critical cargo lift. More important, CRAF probably would not have been implemented without a declaration of a state of emergency, which would have placed additional new demands on the entire logistical system.

It was unrealistic to expect that 143 million ton-miles would have been allocated because JCS refused to grant any preallocations for Army use. Yet the Department of the Army (DA) hoped for these assets and "failed to

---

*A ton-mile is the lift capacity necessary to carry 2,000 pounds one mile. It would take one million ton-miles to carry 1,000 tons 1,000 miles.

8

give adequate considerations to the airlift implications of theater contingency plans."[23] Moreover, theater commanders also had been making plans for the deployment of strong battle groups and supporting elements in similar emergency situations without regard to airlift capabilities. These problems eventually forced JCS to decide which of the contingency plans were to be implemented and to assign the lift resources accordingly.[24] Basically, it appeared that MATS did have sufficient airlift for contingency operations, but this total airlift proved to be unsatisfactory because of service priorities, theater requirements, operational commitments, and misleading aggregate totals (by including CRAF).

What MATS lacked in quantity was not made up in quality. The C-124 aircraft in 1958 (134 in regular MATS service) could carry 12.5 tons for 3,000 miles, but they were rapidly approaching obsolescence. MATS had twenty C-133 aircraft that could carry twenty-six tons over 4,000 miles.[25] At the time of the operations in Lebanon, the 322d Air Division in Germany had forty-eight C-130s, forty-eight C-124s, and fifty C-119s available (table 1).[26]

Table 1. Aircraft Capability

Type	Range (miles)/Speed (mph)	Payload (lbs)
C-124	1,232/272	56,000 (200 trps with fld equip)
C-119	1,950-2,280/200	27,500 (67 trps)
C-130	2,880/330	25,800 (64 trps)
	1,940/335	39,400
	2,760/335	31,500
C-133A	4,030	50,000
	1,300	100,000

Source: *Jane's All the World's Aircraft, 1957-1958* (New York: McGraw-Hill Book Co., 1958).

The Military Sea Transportation Service (MSTS) was in somewhat better condition. The Army was still MSTS's biggest customer, although it was moving toward air passenger service more and more. Given available sealift, the surface elements of the lead division force and the full follow-on division force could possibly be in the objective area within 30 days "but not necessarily unloaded."[27] The main problem was the long time required for conventional shipping to load and discharge cargo. The Army was aware of the problem and had long been researching different methods of cargo handling. Roll-on and roll-off ships provided one solution. In 1954, Congress authorized DOD to purchase roll-on and roll-off vessels, and, in January 1958, the first of these, the USNS Comet, was put into service in Europe. Heavy vehicles and armor could drive directly on or off this ship instead of being loaded or unloaded by a crane.

JCS was confident in MSTS's capability. By JCS calculations, "hot bunking" (two men to a bunk on a shift basis) could meet contingency operations. Accordingly, JCS authorized a reduction of the MSTS active troop fleet in fiscal year 1959 to 23 ships (table 2). That this number, many on worldwide service, could not immediately provide enough available ships for troop lift was all too evident in the Middle East crisis.[28]

Table 2. Selected Ship Capability

Type	Speed (knots)	Payload
Upshur/Geiger	19-20	1,896 trps
General G. M. Randall	20	5,500 trps
Comet	18	700 vehs (two holds fwd for gen cgo)

Source: Jane's Fighting Ships, 1957-1958 (New York: McGraw-Hill Book Co., 1957).

Plans

Since the mid-1950s, the Army Staff had been involved in planning for contingency operations in the Middle East and, by spring 1956, had a deployment plan designed to deter or halt hostilities between Israel and an Arab state. This plan, Swaggerstick, consisted of having a two-division force of STRAC units (approximately 16,939 personnel) airlifted in approximately fifteen days to an overseas terminal. Logistical support would come from the

United States and designated overseas areas.[29] Swaggerstick was never submitted to JCS for approval or allocation of resources. Therefore, "Army planning for the strategic lift of its 'Swaggerstick' forces was largely speculative."[30] In the end, it was the question of inadequate strategic lift that canceled Swaggerstick in favor of a theater plan.

The Egyptian-Israeli crisis in the spring of 1956 prompted JCS to direct the Commander in Chief, Naval Element, Mediterranean (CINCNELM), to initiate contingency plans at the theater level.[31] (See figure 4.) On receipt of orders, CINCNELM would become CINCSPECOMME. From the beginning, this plan called for a joint effort: the Sixth Fleet would provide Marines for initial landings; the Commander in Chief, U.S. Air Force, Europe (CINCUSAFE), would organize and deploy an air task force; MSTS would provide the sealift; MATS, as directed by JCS, would provide the airlift augmentation to CINCUSAFE; and the Commander in Chief, Europe (CINCEUR), would be directed to provide the necessary forces to implement these plans. The Army requirement would be provided from U.S. Army, Europe (USAREUR), and would consist initially of a regimental-size task force from the 9th Infantry Division. When the 11th Airborne Division arrived in Europe in 1956, it received the 9th's mission because of its airland or airborne capability. The 11th Airborne Division was shortly designated the 24th Infantry Division, but its two designated airborne battle groups remained part of this contingency plan. These airborne battle groups and support units selected from available USAREUR COMMZ units (later to become the 201st Logistical Command) totaled over 10,000 men and became Army Task Force 201.

One CINCNELM contingency plan for the Middle East, code-named Bluebat, called for a combined operation of British and U.S. forces. The unilateral U.S. portion of Bluebat, CINCSPECOMME Operation Plan (OPLAN) 215-58, provided for initial action by Marine units followed by Army forces. Supporting plans developed by subordinate headquarters were Emergency Plan 201 (EP 201) for USAREUR, 24th Infantry Division's plan in support of EP 201, and that division's load-out and marshaling plan called Grandios.*

Based on these plans, Brig. Gen. David W. Gray, assistant division commander of the 24th Infantry Division, became the commanding general for ATF 201.

---

*Appendix A contains a summary of the plans developed.

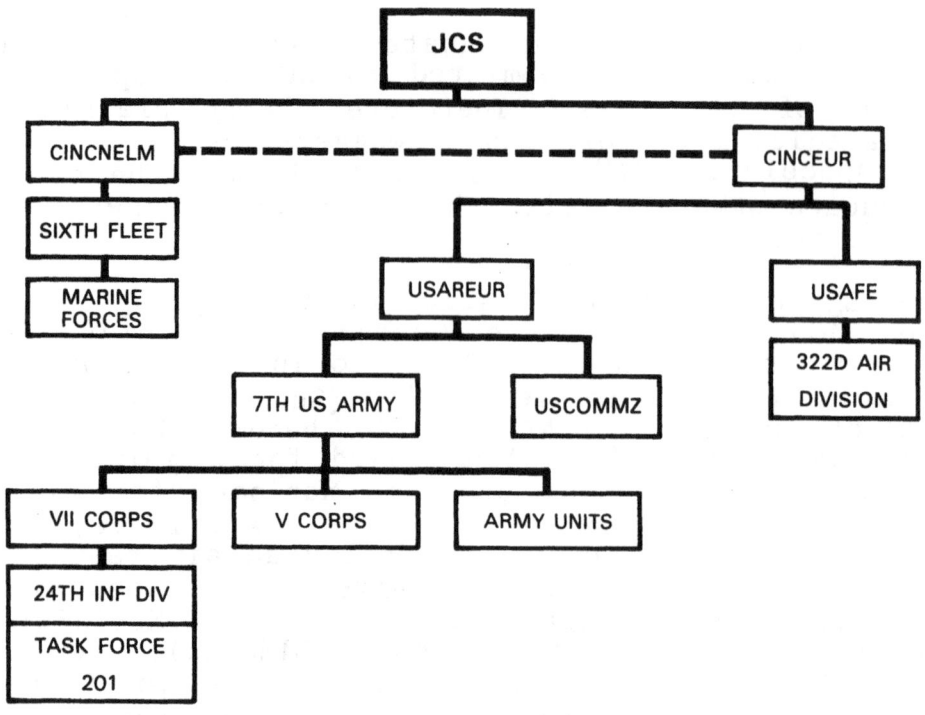

Source: "Infantry Conference Report," Comments, 210.
Figure 4. Organization for Planning

General Gray, while assigned to the DA staff, had worked on the original Swaggerstick plan. Assigned to USAREUR in 1958, he would have to "execute a mission at a lower level which he [had] helped conceive at a higher level."32 Because Bluebat was a joint effort, planning conferences were necessary to enable future participants to become acquainted with each other's problems and techniques. In December 1957, the 24th Infantry Division headquarters hosted a three-day conference for representatives of all echelons of command from all three services. A conference wargame required an airborne assault to seize a specific airfield in a Middle Eastern country. Players wargamed every phase of the operation and, for the first time, carefully analyzed logistical requirements. According to General Gray, "this wargame did more than anything to put our planning on a sound, realistic basis."33

Such a meeting was imperative due to the multitude of headquarters involved and their disparate locations.* For example, CINCNELM was located in London; European Command (EUCOM), Paris; USAREUR, Heidelberg; Seventh Army,

---

*There were at least twelve headquarters or agencies (JCS, DA, DCSLOG, CONUS, CINCNELM, EUCOM, USAREUR COMMZ, USAREUR, SETAF, 24th Infantry Division, MSTS, MATS) that had to coordinate in implementing the logistical plan.

Stuttgart; 11th Airborne Division, near Stuttgart; COMMZ, Orléans, France; U.S. Port, Bremerhaven; 12th Air Force, Ramstein; and the 322d Air Division, Évreux, France. Officers identified more than 100 problems, and "periodic followups were made so that by time of deployment most of the problems had been resolved."[34] Colonel Meetze recalled that these conferences introduced the teamwork that was so essential to any type of operation.[35]

The Army portion of Bluebat, USAREUR EP 201, called for military forces to seize the Beirut-Ruzaq-Estabel area by airdropping and/or airlanding Army forces, by initiating an amphibious assault of the Marine battalion landing team, or by combining both methods. Basically, the forces were to deter or stop hostilities between Israel and Arab states, restore order and stability, assure the independence of a sovereign state, protect American lives and property in that state, and provide CINCSPECOMME with an Army task force reinforced with minimum essential combat and combat service support elements. The first tangible task of the force would be to obtain and develop airfields and facilities. USAREUR had to:

- Provide the logistical support to ATF 201 until resupply from CONUS was established.

- Continue to furnish emergency resupply.

- Provide staff augmentation for CINCSPECOMME.

- Provide emergency replacements for ATF 201.

- Establish a USAREUR movement coordination center.

- Provide, upon request by CINCUSAFE, an engineer construction company to the air task force.[36]

USAREUR and CONUS shared logistical support for the force. Section IV and annex D to EP 201 gave specific logistical instructions. Logistical support for ATF 201 would be provided by USAREUR until E+30 days,* after which DA would assume that responsibility. CINCUSAFE also had to provide emergency class I support and support for the advance party. EP 201 stated that the sea tail arriving from USAREUR COMMZ on E+20 would bring all classes of supply for the entire ATF 201 within prescribed levels. The first DA resupply was slated to arrive at E+35

---

*E-day was the day on which execution of deployment was ordered by higher headquarters.

days.37   Here was a good place for execution to fall apart because a USAREUR plan was dependent on CONUS for support.

Coordination, however, did occur and the CONUS resupply was ready. Lt. Gen. Carter B. Magruder, Deputy Chief of Staff for Logistics (DCSLOG), DA, emphasized the need for advanced planning, stating "we cannot afford to wait until the movement is ordered to ask for the necessary decisions."38 CONUS support consisted of eleven separate increments, adding up to an estimated 48,767 measurement tons of resupply. In response to General Magruder's initiative, CONUS depots physically prepared the first of the eleven increments of automatic resupply for shipment early in 1958. In addition, stocks were administratively earmarked for later increments, and various other steps were taken to assure the implementation of the established resupply schedule.39 Part of this readiness effort included an unannounced rehearsal of the capability of technical services to resupply ATF 201 automatically. This exercise began on 17 June 1958 and involved the immediate picking, packing, and shipment to terminals of one-half of the first increment of supplies required to support EP 201. By mid-July, when the crisis in Lebanon required execution of EP 201, "virtually all the supplies involved in the exercise had been shipped and were ready for subsequent disposition instructions."40

Army logistical planners in the Pentagon limited the first and second CONUS convoys to class I, III, and V supplies, with only limited II and IV items included.* Repair parts were to be restricted to first- and second-echelon parts. After the second ship convoy from CONUS, class V would be shipped only on call of the commanding general, ATF 201. Routine resupply was to go into effect six months after E-day.41

The Army ground forces to be supported by this resupply effort were identified in EP 201 as a task force divided into five elements, called Alfa, Bravo, Charlie,

---

*In 1958, classes of supply consisted of the following: class I, rations and health and comfort items; class III, petroleum, oils, and lubricants; class V, ammunition; class II, clothing, weapons, and vehicles for which allowances were fixed by TOE; and class IV, equipment and supplies for which allowances were not prescribed or which required special measures of control and were not otherwise classified, such as fortification and construction materials.

Delta, and Echo forces. Alfa and Bravo forces consisted of the airborne combat troops and their organic support; Charlie, Delta, and Echo forces consisted mainly of units from the 201st Logistical Command. (See appendix B for a breakdown of forces.) Alfa and Bravo forces would deploy with class V basic loads to last about ten days and with the minimum of supplies necessary to maintain combat operations until the 201st Logistical Command could establish resupply at about E+3 days. At that time, the first air resupply would arrive with ten days of class I and five days of class III. Additional air resupply would increase supply levels to fifteen days for class I and ten days for class III, and an emergency sea resupply from the Southern European Task Force (SETAF), arriving about E+10 days, would further increase supplies to twenty-five days for class I, twenty days for class III, and ten days for class V. All logistics would be provided on an extremely austere basis, with classes II and IV kept to minimum levels, just sufficient to sustain anticipated operations. If deployed by air, Charlie Force would carry enough supplies for about twenty days. Charlie, Delta, and Echo forces, if deployed by sea, would have minimum accompanying supplies to sustain the forces until the sea resupply from CONUS arrived in the operational area. EP 201 stated that this seaborne shipment was expected to arrive in Turkey at E+20 days and was to contain twenty days of all types of supplies. This plan further stipulated that replacement of supplies was automatically expected when levels dropped to ten days.[42]

EP 201 included plans for a STRAC deployment that would have added an additional fifteen days to the resupply timetable from CONUS, E+45 days as opposed to E+30 days. All the planning for the deployment of a STRAC unit under Swaggerstick had to be redone because the entire force was now to be deployed by sea instead of the initial airlift. This resulted again from a lack of strategic airlift and from how the airlift was allocated to the theater operations.[43]

Problems

Logistical planning for EP 201 was the responsibility of small groups of people. As in other cases, plans and annexes were classified top secret, with a strict need-to-know policy enforced at all times. Excessive security restrictions nullified much of the good work already accomplished in the plans and caused the biggest breakdown in planning for the operation. The logistical portion of EP 201 called for the creation of a type A logistical command to serve as headquarters for the technical and service units selected for ATF 201. These units had already been carefully selected before the mission. But because of the controlled access to EP 201, few of the concerned units knew that they would be deployed. Although these units were technically proficient, they had no idea what they were expected to do, where they were to go, and how many troops they were to support. They had no knowledge of the planners' accomplishments, such as what automatic requisitions the planners had arranged and on what basis they had calculated supply units. Lt. Col. (later Col.) Dan K. Dukes, Jr., chief of plans at Headquarters, USAREUR COMMZ, who later became the deputy commander for the 201st Logistical Command, stated he did not participate in the planning and, in fact, received no briefing or any information concerning the plan. He doubted that many other officers in COMMZ headquarters were informed until shortly before the OPLAN was implemented.44

Moreover, planners followed the contemporary doctrine and formed a logistical command as a focal point for all technical and service functions. They established a push system of supplies via automatic requisitions. But the planners never passed this information on to the technical units that would probably support the operational plans. USAREUR planners prepared requisitions for stocks and repair parts, but the high security classification of the plan precluded units from identifying or earmarking stocks for fear of compromising the mission.45 Colonel Meetze commented:

> The pitfalls in this planning evolved into two segments, with both hampered by the high security involved: First, the selection of units required for the mission, and second, determining the items and quantities of materiel desired and when they should be available. These two segments, of course, include such details as what is a day of supply of the various types of ammunition required for the specific mission involved; how is resupply to be handled (including automatic); what theatre and organizations are to be the backup for supplies and for how long; will it be possible to procure subsistence items in the Operational Theatre, and so on and on. Remember too that coordination was required in the many echelons of command: JCS, CINCSPECOMME, USAREUR COMMZ, etc.
>
> Secrecy prevented us from obtaining valued information from staff specialists and from units which were included in the plan, and determining the quantities of all items required was a tremendous chore. The combat commanders made the

decision of how much ammo and how much food each man would have with him at the time of the initial drop or landing but from then on it was the responsibility of the Support Command. Here is where the cooperation and frequent visits between the combat forces and the logistical command planners really paid dividends. Again, because of the high security of the plan, stocks could not be earmarked or segregated in warehouses or depots. It was only logical then that when the preprogrammed stocks were outloaded from depots to debarkation points on a rush basis that conditions were ripe for a "snafu."[46]

Logistical policies set forth in EP 201 included the provision that no supplies or equipment were to be stockpiled prior to the implementation of the plan. This proved to be a major stumbling block in the coming load-out; moreover, no one, except a small cell of select planners, knew what was supposed to happen, and, of course, no one knew when it would happen.

CHAPTER 2

THE DEPLOYMENT

Preparation

The primary function of logistics is to sustain a force during operations away from its base. Planners for deployment, whether they realize it or not, are logisticians. In the case of ATF 201, plans to implement Bluebat existed for some time. The 11th Airborne Division, a unit designated for Bluebat, was no stranger to deployments and, since March 1956, had been using Grandios, an unclassified deployment plan, to implement EP 201.[1] This plan, written by an experienced staff, called for the marshaling and loading of the airborne maneuver forces.

The primary problem was the dual mission of the division--its commitment to NATO and to EP 201. General Gray related that he developed "a mild case of schizophrenia and was never really satisfied that [he] was doing full justice to either mission."[2] Additionally, the Army organized the 11th Airborne Division under the Reorganization of the Airborne Division (ROTAD) concept. To complicate matters further, the 11th Airborne Division was about to undergo a major change in force structure and would become the 24th Infantry Division on 1 July 1958 as part of the Reorganization of Current Infantry Division (ROCID) model.[3] ROCID increased its equipment and personnel and added another brigade headquarters.[4] Two battle groups within the division, the 187th and 503d, would retain their airborne capability. Late in 1958, these units would rotate to Fort Bragg, North Carolina, and two infantry battle groups would come from the United States to replace them. Simultaneously, two airborne battle groups from Fort Bragg, the 504th and 505th, would replace two infantry battle groups in the 8th Division at Mainz, West Germany. "When this rotation occurred the 8th Division was to assume the TF 201 mission."[5] In the meantime, personnel approaching the end of their overseas tour filled the 187th and 503d. As a result, both ATF 201 battle groups "were jam-packed with officers, NCOs and other ranks who had all served three years in Germany and had participated in numerous major field exercises and training tasks."[6]

A small staff in the division continued the EP 201 planning in spite of having to prepare for two different missions and to deal with the turbulence of a major reorganization and massive personnel rotation. These planners had to develop a plan to marshal and load out 4,963 troops and 2,604 short tons of equipment. (See appendix C.) Because of the complexity of marshaling and the numbers of personnel involved, all units involved had to understand the plan. But Grandios was a plan solely for the airborne units, and it neglected detailed planning for the nondivisional support units.

The marshaling of an airborne unit is a time-consuming and labor-intensive operation. It involves the establishment of a departure airfield control group. Control group personnel must provide transportation and establish messing, latrine, and sleeping areas for the troops at the departure airfield, plus handle such duties as sealing off the area for security, providing guards, and setting up command and briefing tents. A second group of personnel has to establish and operate a marshaling area to process airborne personnel and their equipment for loading. Adjutant general, ordnance, maintenance, and quartermaster personnel need to be stationed in the marshaling area to provide last-minute administrative services; to check identification cards, shot records, and Geneva Convention cards, to notify next of kin; to perform myriad personnel matters; and to repair and replace equipment. The division believed that the plan for marshaling procedures was workable. Then came a real test.[7]

Growing tensions in the Middle East caused an alert to be called on 17 May 1958. At that time, the 503d Battle Group was the designated Alfa Force. This alert added realism to the paper contingency plan and exposed serious errors that would require major revisions in future planning. Both the 187th and the 503d marshaled according to plan. Planners soon discovered, however, that there were not enough people to process the battle groups quickly. Their planning also failed to marshal the units effectively because of a lack of control and coordination among the various support units. The alert ended on 24 May when the 503d conducted a mass airdrop near Munich, Germany. This alert, however, clearly demonstrated that the task force could not then move at the speed required in actual contingency operations.[8]

As long as the 11th Division remained an airborne unit, it was simple to detail individuals and units familiar with airborne marshaling and departure tasks. As the division gradually converted to an infantry unit, it lost its airborne personnel (other than the 187th and 503d) and also lost much of its ability to marshal its units quickly and effectively.

To overcome this deficiency, Major General Ralph C. Cooper, CG 11th Airborne Division, tasked Brigadier General George Speidel, 11th Division Artillery Commander, to operate the departure airfield. In addition to his long experience as a paratrooper, General Speidel was stationed at Fürstenfeldbruck near Munich. He supervised all the division troops located in the Munich area and could draw on their resources for his task force. Furthermore, as an assistant division commander, he could make decisions and resolve problems more quickly than could an officer of lesser rank.[9]

This force become known as Support Force Speidel. Its mission was "to provide for the movement of task force and supporting elements from home station, by air, for commitment in an area of operations, or to an intermediate staging area."[10]

Grandios, upon implementation, reorganized the division as shown in figure 5. Support Force Speidel was the heart of Grandios. The personnel included one battle group, two infantry battalions, an artillery battalion, and one engineer battalion (figures 6 and 7). The plan defined responsibilities for all the required marshaling tasks, such as providing guidance for supply loads, individual equipment, vehicle preparation, public information, communications, and even special services like post exchange and movies at the marshaling area.[11]

After the practice in May, the alert system became more precise and graduated as shown in table 3. The airborne force now had workable procedures for deployment, and coordination continued for possible deployment. Problems still remained for the support elements of ATF 201. Because of the security classification of EP 201, the 11th Airborne Division could not provide details of the plan to the support units that would constitute the 201st Logistical Command. In short, logistical units could not be integrated into the operational plans. Consequently, the working units did not have an opportunity to prepare loading plans, movement schedules, or airfield departure routes. According to an after-action report, coordination and review of the air-loading plans for nondivisional Charlie Force units were not effected prior to the alert, and detailed loading plans for the Delta and Echo forces were not coordinated with the port of embarkation.[12] Only a small cell of headquarters planners fully understood the nature of the requirement. Detailed planning for these units began only after a relaxation of the need-to-know restriction placed on EP 201, but this was less than a month and a half before the actual deployment in July. The plans for the

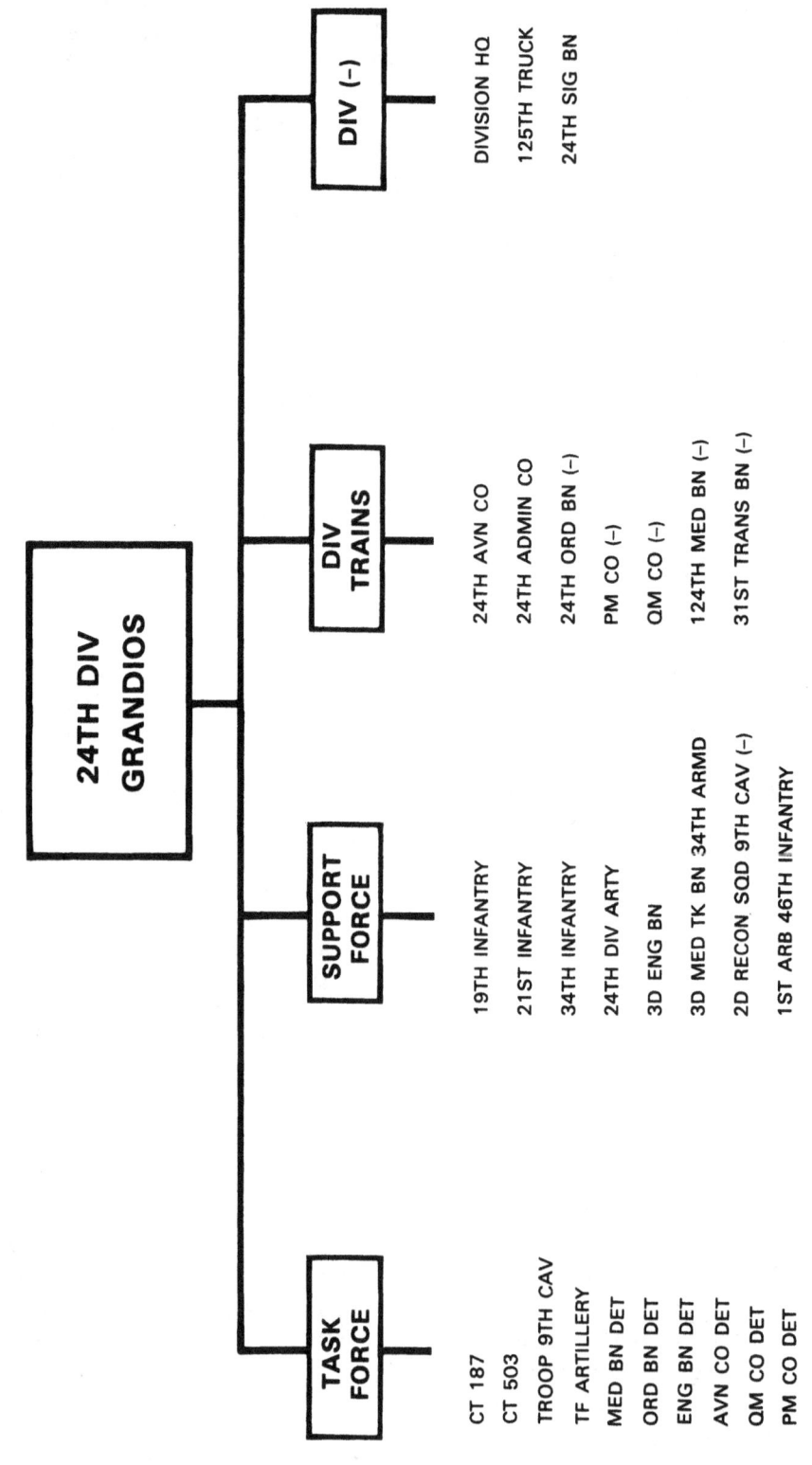

Source: "Infantry Conference Report," Comments, 220.

Figure 5. Organization for Operation Grandios

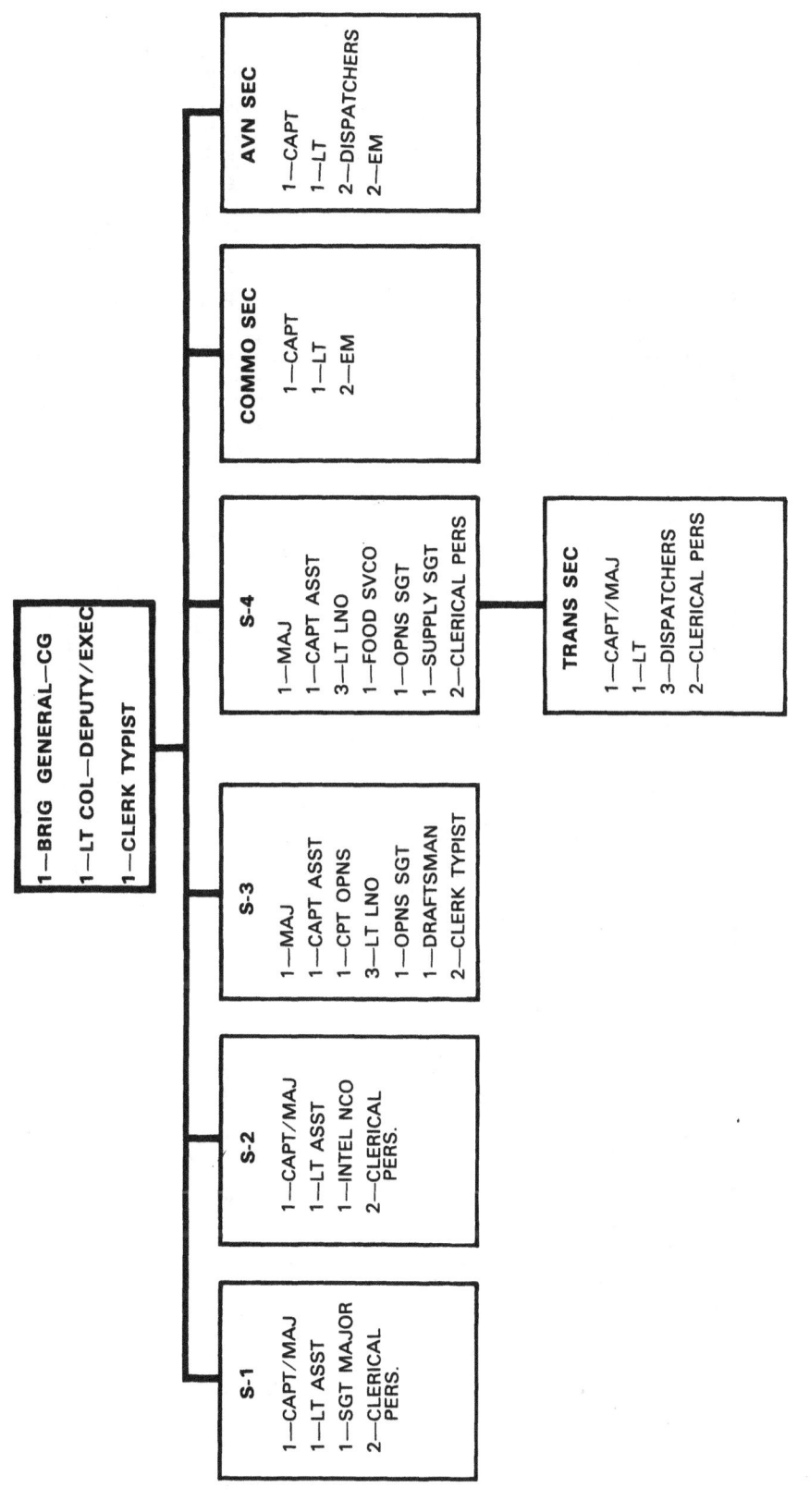

Source: 24th ID, "AAR Grandios," with enclosure, "Operation Plan GRANDIOS," 1 July 1958, annex E.

Figure 6. Support Force

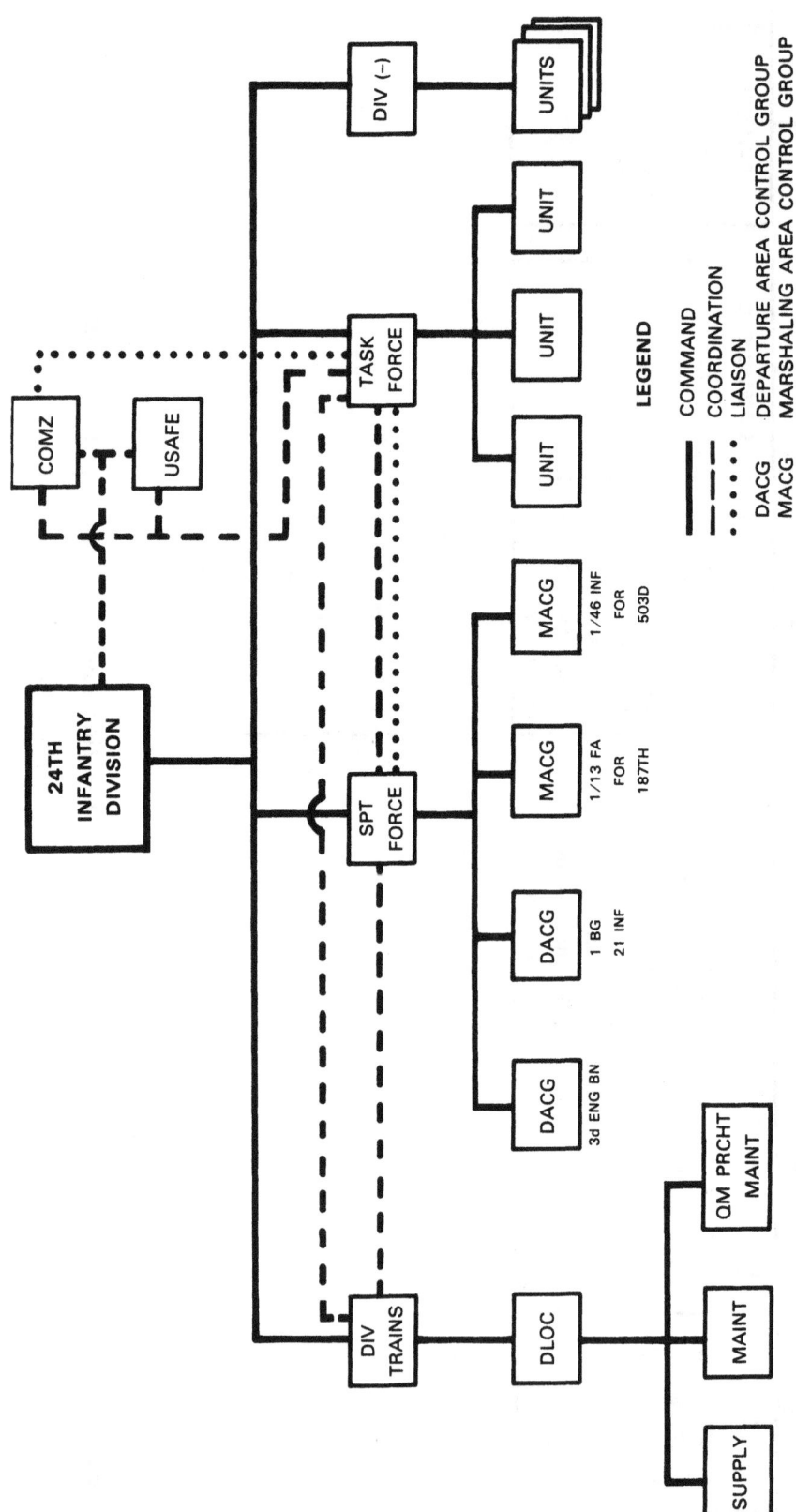

Source: 24th ID, "AAR Grandios," with enclosure, "Operation Plan GRANDIOS," 1 July 1958, annex C.

Figure 7. Command Organization for Operation Grandios

Table 3. Types of Alerts

Amber	Azure	Green	Purple
An alert or warning order has been received from higher headquarters, but the situation appears to warrant minimum alert procedures.	Higher headquarters has issued a warning but has emphasized that this does not constitute an alert.	This constitutes an actual alert. Task force prepares to move to departure airfield(s).	This constitutes a full alert. All aspects of Grandios will be executed. All measures applicable to Amber, Azure, and Green alerts will be accomplished.
1. Review plans. 2. Determine whereabouts of key personnel. 3. Determine major shortages.	1. Accomplish measures applicable to Amber alert. 2. Approve no leaves. 3. Return units to home station. 4. Restrict 3-day passes. 5. Conduct showdown inspections. 6. Make up shortages. 7. Prepare personnel transfer lists.	1. Accomplish measures applicable to Amber and Azure. 2. Execute Grandios muster. 3. Set up rigging lines. 4. Execute personnel and equipment transfers. 5. Ascertain aircraft available. 6. Install communications. 7. Cancel all leaves and passes. 8. Administer immunizations.	

Source: "Infantry Conference Report," Comments, 221.

movement were sound and the forces were deployed, but a smoother deployment could have been possible. The airborne planning was thorough, but restricted distribution of the plan resulted in faulty execution.

The logistical command leadership understood the mission and held many planning conferences. Colonel Meetze even made a liaison trip to Adana, Turkey, the proposed intermediate staging area, to coordinate logistical support.[13] While the headquarters was becoming well versed in the prepared plan, the specific support units were not. Unlike the airborne units, the nondivisional support units lacked the experience for rapid deployment and thus required extensive preparation and planning. They did not receive it because of the high security classification of the plan.

The lessons of the May alert helped to integrate support units into the detailed marshaling plans. General Gray described the outcome:

> . . . another result was that it let the cat out of the bag, that a U.S. NATO force had a secondary mission. As I recall, the main reason for the extreme "need to know" imposed upon us was the concern that our allies, and particularly West Germany, might find out that the U.S. planned to use forces fully committed to NATO on a distant mission. As it turned out the only concern expressed by anyone was that of German entrepreneurs who stood to lose revenues upon departure of U.S. forces. In all probability, despite our precautions, NATO knew about it all along, to say nothing of the Russians.[14]

The May alert finally brought Charlie Force units into the detailed planning picture. For the first time, these units calculated airlift data and prepared loading plans, but, reflecting their inexperience, they had to rely heavily on the airborne units for help. An 8 July command post exercise (CPX) for all Charlie Force units accelerated this process, but units were still unprepared when deployment came.[15]

After the May alert, the Air Force agreed to furnish a component to a joint command post at Fürstenfeldbruck to coordinate aircraft and provide advance notice of types of arriving aircraft.[16] The Air Force, however, had difficulty forecasting aircraft by type. The replacement of C-119s with C-130s, then in progress, caused this confusion. As General Gray related, "it was impossible for the Air Force to give us at any one time an accurate forecast of their potential lift."[17]

In the wake of the experiences gained from the May alert, airlift was again the subject of a 9 July 12th Air Force conference at Ramstein, Germany. Brig. Gen. B. O. Davis said to General Gray, "We gave you what you asked for in May and now you want more. When are you going to stop raising the ante?" General Gray replied that General Davis had been misinformed because "TF Alfa's requirement had been met only by taking C-124 augmentation from the States meant for TF Charlie." General Gray has recalled, "The simple fact was that there was not enough lift immediately available in the theater to meet the full lift requirements of TF Alpha."[18] The difference between requirements and lift availability remained unresolved.

Planning and coordination continued. ATF 201 was fortunate to have had the benefit of CPXs, rehearsals, and marshaling and load-out practices. Charlie Force was now involved in the planning, and the Army and Air Force were discussing joint planning. The May full-dress rehearsal revealed areas where corrective action was necessary, but those involved had too little time--only a month and a half--before the next alert to correct the problems.

On 14 July 1958, USAREUR issued a warning order by phone to the 24th Division headquarters; on 15 July, a "message [arrived] from USAREUR which indicated that the task force would have to be prepared for either air drop or air land in Lebanon 24 hours after receipt of notification to move."[19] The same day, USAREUR General Order Number 194 activated the ATF 201 Support Command headquarters.[20] General Speidel activated his force and moved to Fürstenfeldbruck Air Force Base. The first task of the headquarters was to determine lift availability.

Movement

On 14 July, the 322d Air Division had available forty-eight C-130 aircraft from the 317th Troop Carrier Wing at Évreux, France; twelve C-124 aircraft from the 322d Division's 3d Troop Carrier Squadron at Rhine-Main, West Germany; fifty C-119 aircraft from the division's 60th Troop Carrier Wing based at Dreux, France; and thirty-six C-124s turned over to the 322d by MATS Eastern Air Transport Force.[21] The next day, General Gray again met with General Davis, 12th Air Force, and Colonel McCafferty, deputy commander of the 322d Air Division (322d was commanded by Col. Clyde Box), to receive an estimate of the airlift available for his mission. General Gray recorded in his personal notebook that "final airlift [was] not formed up until about 2000."[22] Gray elaborated: "In fairness to the Air Force, the 322d was

Troops leaving Germany

sort of a vagabond airline that on any one day might have aircraft scattered all the way from India to Africa to the United States. They simply couldn't all be whistled in in a matter of a few hours. . . ."23

Like the Air Force, Army elements were prepared for contingencies but were not ready for an unannounced alert because of their attention to daily operations. Most soldiers familiar with alert situations would have empathy for ATF 201's quandry. Despite the contingency mission, the units had to do other jobs and continue training. On 14 July, for instance, the 503d, designated Alfa Force, was preparing to depart for Bad Tölz to act as aggressors against special forces troops in an exercise. They were also in the midst of readying a company-size jump for Gen. Clyde D. Eddleman, the new Seventh Army commander. This task required the rigging of several dummy demonstration loads.24 On the other hand, the 187th (Bravo Force) had just returned to garrison from two weeks' training at Hohenfels where it had conducted a group jump. Before its departure from home station, the 187th reviewed its portion of Grandios and readied its B-bags, which contained an individual's clothing, some designated TOE equipment, and some personal items. Preparing for his portion of the special forces exercises, Colonel Sharkey, the 187th's commander, sent many of his officers to reconnoiter the operational area. At that moment, they were scattered over a 200-square-mile area of the Bavarian Alps. In addition, Colonel Haynes, the Alfa Force commander, had injured his leg in a recent jump. Based on these factors, General Gray replaced the 503d with the 187th as the Alfa Force.[25] At 0545 on 15 July, the division initiated a green alert, and the 187th began loading.

By this time, Support Force Speidel had established the departure airfield control group. General Speidel recalled, "During marshaling and loading many minor problems occurred which were corrected without too much difficulty. This was a standard operating procedure that had been 'dry run' many times."[26]

The most nettlesome minor problem was the Air Force's failure to send the required airmen to the joint command post as previously agreed on during the 9 July conference.[27] The American Land Forces (AMLANFOR) Bluebat critique mistakenly states: "They [the Air Force] furnished one officer; however, he departed in the increment with the ATF 201 Commander. This caused much confusion and delay in aircraft use and in briefings until an Air Force component, with command and clerks, was re-established much later."[28] In actuality, the Air Force officer, Colonel McCafferty, was the designated commander of the Air Force element of Alfa Force while airborne. If the 187th had to jump, McCafferty would have been in command en route to the target area.[29] The Air Force did send additional personnel. A combat air logistic support unit (CALSU), under Col. Tarleton H. Watkins, worked with General Speidel, but not according to any prior agreements.[30] The result was confusion and lack of coordination. The Army contributed its share to this disorder by its last-minute scramble to complete loading plans for Charlie Force.

The mission of Support Force Speidel was soon modified to include the establishment of priorities for movement and the determination of lift requirements for all units in ATF 201. This meant supporting not only the well-prepared airborne units but also the nondivisional support units, many of which had just recently been included in the plans.[31] This presented a significant problem. As a plan, EP 201 was sound, but the loading requirements of the support units had not been computed. Many of these units, reporting increased lift requirements for the first time, expected Support Force Speidel to react immediately to their needs. However, unless cleared by higher headquarters, Support Force Speidel and the 322d Air Division headquarters lacked authority to dispatch aircraft other than those contained in the basic plan.32 Despite the previous months of preparation, it required a great deal of last-minute coordination and telephone calls to rectify the aircraft shortfall.

Another of General Speidel's problems was all the "help" he received.33 It is a truism that senior commanders have the right, possibly the need, to go where the action is and to expect a briefing on their arrival. But the price is interruption of the operation in progress. General Gray counted fourteen stars in one group. "At one time there was General Hodes, CGUSAREUR; LTG Eddleman; LTG Roger; MG Cooper; and BG B. O. Davis."34 General Gray erected a briefing tent to keep the visitors away from Speidel's workers, but the generals avoided the briefing area and wandered over to the hangars, asking questions that a briefing officer could have answered and interfering with troops engaged in more important duties. Indicative of events to come, only Gen. Paul D. Adams, Commanding General, 7th Support Command, listened to a complete briefing.35 (General Adams later became Commander in Chief, AMLANFOR.)

Besides visitors, General Speidel's force was unprepared to handle the press. Apparently, there was no fixed policy for press accommodations. For example:

> Two representatives from the "Stars and Stripes" arrived by an Army helicopter from Frankfurt (Germany) with orders issued by "Stars and Stripes" for travel to the Middle East. This headquarters (Support Force Speidel) had no authority to allow them aboard aircraft based simply on their "Stars and Stripes" orders. The Information Division, USAREUR, was contacted. . . . Eventually, 22 July, this headquarters was notified through Division PIO that these men had no authority to go to the Middle East and in fact should not even be on the base proper. Yet these same two men were provided Army helicopter transportation from Frankfurt to Fürstenfeldbruck, and had USAFE approval for air transportation to the Middle East. Good press relations are a necessity for favorable releases concerning the military profession. A policy, known to all, must be forthcoming in relation to the access of press representatives to sensitive areas.36

To add insult to injury, "Even the Russians," General Gray noted, "were at the fence taking pictures."37 The result was an unplanned diversion of additional personnel and resources to handle the demands of the press, thus allowing troops to deal with the problems at hand.

Plans and weight estimates did not match the actual loads, creating further difficulties. Nearly every element of the well-practiced Alfa Force had overloaded its equipment bundles. In addition, the operation was delayed from the start. Riggers incorrectly loaded the truck convoy by putting the items needed initially on the ground into the trucks first; therefore, that equipment was unloaded last. The convoy also took a longer route than necessary to the airfield and arrived late and in reverse order. The riggers then had to wait until the last truck arrived with the materiel needed first before they could begin their work.

On 15 July, these riggers in the parachute maintenance company moved to the airfield at 0500. But it took until 1600 to establish the rigging line. At 1800, when the force received clearance to depart, only the first of 125 heavy drop-loads were ready.[38] Fortunately, the weather delayed the departure of the C-119s as did the failure to receive overflight rights from Austria.* These factors forced departure time to be rescheduled for 0730 the next day.

ATF 201 continued to marshal. Fortunately, it had a unique headquarters staff, Support Force Speidel, that consisted of experienced personnel and a general officer to operate the departure airfield. Thus, effective organization and well-qualified people helped overcome some of the attendant confusion. However, even with thorough preparation and experienced personnel, ATF 201 was not ready when cleared for departure.

The first Alfa Force plane actually departed Germany at 0817 on 16 July for Adana, Turkey, a staging area (map 2). Meantime, Charlie Force was also marshaling in France. Because Charlie Force would use Alpha Force's turnaround aircraft, Charlie Force had time to reorganize. Col. Adam W. Meetze, commander of the 201st Logistical Command, Lt. Col. Isaac King, director of supply and services, and Maj. Paul I. Wells, a signal officer, left Orléans, France, and joined General Gray at Adana on 17 July to coordinate logistics.[39] Colonel Meetze immediately supported ATF 201 with B-rations, tents, tables, chairs, and other expendable supplies from

---

*The need for overflight rights had been considered by USAREUR planners, but it was decided that, where they were not granted, they would be ignored. Evidently, the State Department had not cleared this decision because Austria had to be bypassed.

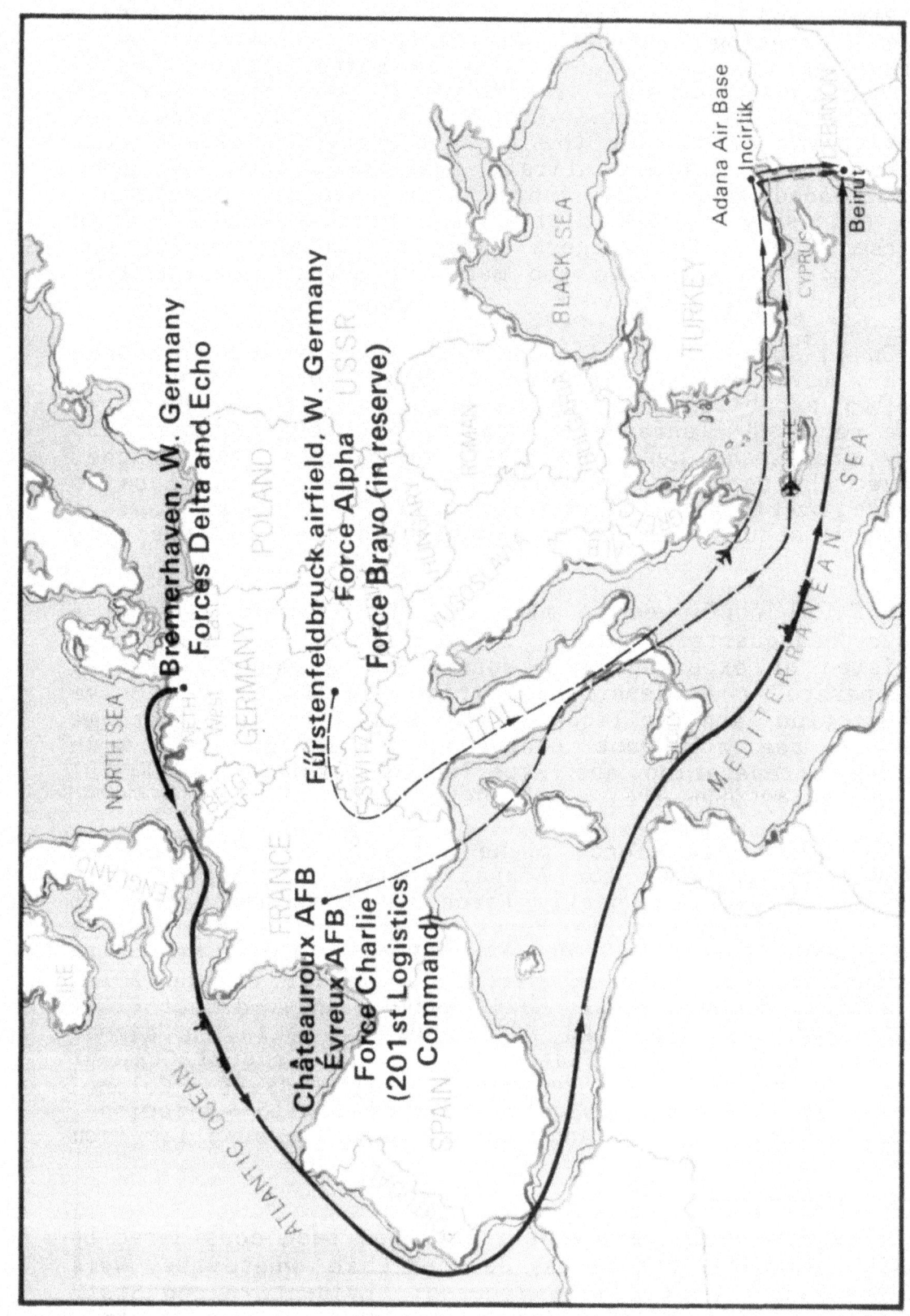

Source: "Infantry Conference Report," Comments, 218.
Map 2. ATF 201 Deployment Routes to Lebanon in 1958

pre-positioned Air Force supplies at Adana. Meanwhile, the airlift continued. By 17 July, a total of 1,526 troops in Alfa Force and 495 short tons of supplies had arrived at Adana, Turkey.[40] Most of these aircraft parked on the airfield, fully loaded. Bravo Force remained on alert at its home station in Germany.*

In Lebanon, the situation was stable, so Charlie Force prepared to land directly at the Beirut airport. Elements of Charlie Force left Orléans, France, by bus on 17 July for the airfield at Châteauroux. Unfortunately, the bus crashed near Olivet (Loiret), France, killing three men.[41] Headquarters, COMMZ, sent replacements who had no notion of the plan they would implement. The rest of the air elements of Charlie Force marshaled without incident at Fürstenfeldbruck, Rhine-Main, Châteauroux, and Évreux.

General Gray visited Beirut on 18 July to prepare the way for the task force. After coordination meetings with Admiral Holloway, CINCSPECOMME, Gray returned to Adana. There, he ordered two changes based on the situation in Lebanon: first, "that a truck platoon be placed as top priority on TF Charlie and [second] that TF Alfa's B-bags be sent by air rather than by sea."[42] Unfortunately, the last request was garbled in transmission. The 24th Division interpreted the message to mean that Bravo Force should advance. So a few days later, the advance party of the 503d arrived in Beirut, happy as could be. The end of this story is that Alfa's B-bags, which went by ship anyway, were extensively damaged and looted on the sea voyage.[43]

On 18 July, USAREUR cleared Charlie Force for movement to Lebanon, and Alfa Force prepared to move on to Beirut. General Gray earlier found that Lebanese airport officials insisted on integrating the task force flights with their normal civilian traffic control. The Beirut airport had two main runways, but one was closed for construction. Gray made arrangements with Lebanese officials for equipment storage and use of Lebanese army trucks, but, when he and the advance party arrived, "to our dismay we found that the Lebanese Army trucks promised us had not arrived; the taxiway had not been reserved and no space

---

*The reader may wonder about the care of family members left behind. Support Force Speidel took care of most of the problems. General Speidel briefed the family members, and his staff took care of many problems caused by a spouse's quick departure, such as "He took the keys to the car."

had been allocated for our heavy drop." The advance party's "high-pressure staff activity" solved all these problems just as the first group of C-119s appeared in the distance.[44]

Alfa Force began arriving in Beirut at 2230 on 19 July; some of Charlie Force had landed earlier that same day. But because Alpha Force was using many of the aircraft Charlie Force had counted on for transport, much of Charlie Force was delayed. In addition, it took longer to load Charlie Force than anticipated: unit planners had manifested vehicles according to the basic weight of the vehicle, but, when the vehicles arrived at the aircraft for loading, they frequently contained rations or other items of equipment that added more weight to the load without appearing on the manifest.[45] So, as aircraft became available, riggers loaded them with whatever was available and sent the aircraft on their way. The bulk of Charlie Force, 1,580 personnel and 1,825 short tons of equipment and supplies, had arrived at Beirut by 26 July. In all, during the first eleven days of the Army's movement, the Air Force flew a total of 242 sorties carrying 3,234 troops and 2,500 short tons of cargo.[46]

187th arriving in Beirut

Airhead

The first priority of the logistical command was air terminal operations. The unloading of airborne units was no problem. The ATF commander, General Gray, described the airborne's airlanding:

> As each aircraft turned into the taxiway still rolling at considerable speed, a soldier jumped off and sprinted forward to establish an assembly point for his plane load. The other soldiers came tumbling out behind him while the plane was still rolling, neatly stacked their weapons and equipment in a line designated by the guide, then raced back to the plane to unload the A-7 containers and weapons bags. In a matter of several minutes the plane was proceeding to the runway for takeoff.[47]

The unloading of supplies and heavy equipment was not as smooth, however. Evidently, considerable confusion existed about who was in charge of unloading. All the services used the Beirut International Airport as their air terminal. In addition, the international airport would eventually serve, on a continuing basis, as the main base of operations for helicopter, light plane, aeromedical evacuation, and antisubmarine warfare operations. All these military activities were superimposed on the constant, heavy commercial use of the airfield. The initial contacts between U.S. and Lebanese officials to coordinate air traffic consisted of little more than a Lebanese army officer and a U.S. Marine representative working with civilians to control landings and takeoffs. During the initial Army airlift, the Air Force provided a CALSU of the 6th Aerial Port Squadron. This unit attempted to control and coordinate all U.S. activities until the arrival of an aeromedical evacuation detachment. Then, the CALSU established a passenger and cargo operations area in the terminal. While these personnel made a commendable effort to carry this extra workload and did manage to operate a limited military base operations center, their numbers and technical ratings were not adequate to handle all airport and terminal activities.[48]

Confusing instructions exacerbated the problem. CINCSPECOMME OPLAN 215-58 stated that Commander, U.S. Air Forces, SPECOMME, would establish and operate air transport facilities to improve the handling of personnel and cargo and to arrange for use of the commercial air transport terminal.[49] A military regulation

(AR 59-106/OPNAV Instruction 4660.1/AFR 76-7/MARCUR JSAR 2-56-3000, 21 September 1956) delineated the functional responsibilities of the military services in connection with handling and moving traffic through Air Force air terminals, including those at advanced landing fields and airheads. Responsibilities differed somewhat for the air movement of units and the air movement of other traffic, such as cargo, mail, passengers, and baggage.

For air movement of units, the respective service (Marine, Navy, Air Force, or Army) being moved was responsible for loading, tying down, and unloading its supplies and equipment into or out of aircraft. Air Force personnel, however, provided technical assistance and safety inspections. In contrast, cargo to be airdropped was tied down and dropped by the Air Force. For movement of traffic other than units, the Air Force was responsible for accepting properly authorized and packaged traffic at the departure air terminals. Acceptance included inspecting, receiving, and unloading traffic from consigner vehicles. The Air Force also had the responsibility of loading, tying down, providing en route service and supervision, unloading, notifying consignees, and delivering traffic at the destination airfield. Delivery at the destination air terminal included loading

Equipment on the runway

traffic on the consignee's vehicles. The Air Force unloading capability at the Beirut airport was insufficient to support an operation of Bluebat's size; therefore, the command pressed combat troops into service as cargo handlers.50

The cargo handling organization consisted of an Air Force team of seven to ten men for each shift; the team unloaded aircraft with two forklift trucks and roller conveyers. The Air Force, however, did not have enough personnel to do the job. The 201st Logistical Command provided a team headed by a transportation officer who supervised the unloading of passengers and cargo. Army combat troops, one officer and twenty men, augmented each of the Air Force shifts.51 Under combat conditions, it is doubtful whether these combat troops could have been spared for that purpose. The movement priority did not infiltrate support troops soon enough to prevent congestion and confusion.

Maritime Operation

As with the airlift, the sealift began almost on time. Because only a single airhead was available and to assure adequate supplies for the task force, the Army loaded two vessels with planned emergency resupply at Leghorn and Brindisi, Italy. On 19 and 20 July, the ships sailed to Beirut, opening the first phase of the sea operation.52

On 20 July, Delta and Echo forces moved to the ports of Bremerhaven, La Pallice, and Saint-Nazaire. In general, rail and highway movements to the ports were effected with minimum disruption of normal traffic flow. At these ports, the men and materiel were promptly loaded, and the first vessel sailed for Beirut on 24 July. This sea tail eventually consisted of 4,862 passengers and 72,011 measurement tons of cargo.53

Before departing for Beirut, Colonel Meetze had sent his S3, Major Kaufmann, to Bremerhaven to supervise the loading of the main elements of Delta and Echo forces on the USS _General Randall_, the USNS _Upshur_, and USNS _Geiger_.54 According to Colonel Meetze, Major Kaufmann had no experience in port operations and was content to let the civilian workers handle the operation.55 Unloading problems resulted in Beirut because the longshoremen did not "combat load" the ships; instead, they loaded the ships "civilian style," even the new roll-on and roll-off vessel, the USNS _Comet_.

Longshoremen at Bremerhaven loaded the Comet with 10,711 measurement tons, "a remarkable lift considering the 'balloon' nature of much of the cargo" (tanks and trucks).[56] Participants estimated that the Comet held the same amount of cargo as four or five World War II Victory ships. The lack of loading ramps and the narrow pier aprons at Bremerhaven, however, prevented roll-on loading, but crane loading took no longer than for conventional vessels. Once aboard, the vehicles were driven to their parking areas.[57] Additional crane-loaded cargo, however, blocked the passageways of the Comet, causing problems at the receiving end because "vehicles had to be lifted out of the vessel before other vehicles could be rolled off."[58]

Two officers and seven enlisted men, the initial Army staff of transportation personnel in Beirut who organized port operations, encountered difficulties while unloading. As described by a staff officer, "failure of operators and staff officers involved in port operations to have knowledge of the overall plans restricted their capabilities to cope with certain facets of the operations."[59] Furthermore, local stevedoring services were not immediately available because of unsettled labor conditions, the language barrier, and certain Lebanese bureaucratic features. Accordingly, initial unloading operations went slowly and would probably not have met the requirements of a combat situation.[60]

Cargo manifests compounded the problem of too few people to carry out the mission. Many manifests were incomplete or missing altogether, and stevedores literally had to unload a ship to discover what was aboard it. For example, no one identified the 299th Engineer Battalion's D-7 bulldozers until 15 August because the shipping manifest listed them as D-8 dozers assigned to the 79th Engineer Construction Battalion.[61]

Conflicting instructions given at home stations for preparing trucks for sea movement caused more problems. Longshoremen removed considerable materiel from truck beds at the port of embarkation to permit efficient storage in the ship holds. They stored the removed materiel without any regard for unit or requirement. On arrival, stevedores unloaded and transported this materiel to assorted dumps where others identified it and shipped it to the proper unit. A dump located at the 299th Engineer Battalion contained communications equipment, ammunition, hospital beds, tents, a fluoroscope, and dump truck headboards. Units had to send labor details to the beach and staging areas to pick up much-needed supplies. Once there, however, the details faced long hours of waiting

Unloading the USNS *Comet*

without any assurance that any of their equipment would be unloaded.62

The 229th Engineer Battalion explained the implications of incorrect cargo manifests:

> The identification of this unit's TAT ["to accompany troops" equipment] was extremely difficult on debarkation from the [USNS] Upshur. A correction to the personnel manifest erroneously awarded a portion of this unit shipment number 74,000 DTX in addition to its correct shipment number 74,000 DMX. Consequently, half of this unit's TAT was marked DMX and the other half DTX. Shipment number 74,000 DTX was shared with the 79th Engineer Construction Battalion which was also aboard the USNS Upshur. As a result, much

General Adams and Colonel Meetze meet the USNS *Upshur*

time was spent opening all shipping boxes marked DTX to determine the rightful owner, and considerable effort was required in double handling much of this equipment. The TAT was loaded in a haphazard manner aboard the ship and was not identifiable by unit on the ship's cargo manifest.63

Once again, faulty execution negated contingency planning.

Result

Problems like incomplete instructions, faulty manifests, and scarce labor could have seriously jeopardized the success of the mission. Unlike the Marine battalion landing teams that arrived ashore with thirty days' combat supplies, Army troops carried a minimum level of supplies. Furthermore, the planned resupply by air was also minimal, as the Army chose to rely on surface resupply. Accordingly, planners should have provided for adequate military personnel to unload MSTS and commercial ships early in the buildup phase. This provision would have allowed Army forces to operate independently of indigenous labor. Personnel for port operations might have been phased into the theater in increments commensurate in size to the off-loading requirements and local labor. In special cases, qualified personnel, such as winch operators, might have accompanied the initial deployment to be readily available as needed at the port.64 Finally, planners should have defined the responsibilities of units more clearly.

Nevertheless, under ATF 201, Americans did deploy to the operational area. In the broad sense, the plan worked. General Gray explained later: "No basic change had to be made in our plan, and such adjustments as were required fell entirely within its framework. On the other hand, we were not loaded and locked within the time frame we had projected and, therefore, did not achieve our objective. In sum, the plan succeeded; we failed in its execution."65 The plans, however, lacked the details necessary for a smooth deployment, such as the confusion nondivisional units had over load-out procedures, incomplete manifests, and cargo loading at the port in Bremerhaven. Other failures in execution resulted because of the high security classification of plans. This was the most significant drawback to well-integrated execution.

CHAPTER 3

THE FULCRUM

A fulcrum is the support on which a lever turns, and combat service support was the fulcrum of rapid deployment logistics for ATF 201. Combat service support propped up this logistical lever sustaining the force by providing resupply and services.

These services are difficult to discuss as a single issue because of the specific nature of each. But these somewhat interdependent services were organized in a single logistical command. Their combat service support functions need to be examined, and the following separate, but related, sections describe certain ones. The chapter begins with a discussion of the organizational process that orients the service support mission. Following sections then discuss resupply; procurement; civil affairs; medical support; and, finally, security, a common problem of all service support units.

Organization

Because the Lebanese operation was a unilateral action, the JCS directive executing the U.S. portion of Bluebat (CINCAMBRITFOR OPLAN 1-58) substituted U.S. forces for British units. This action resulted in the creation of two sizable provisional organizations--one Marine, one Army--each commanded by a brigadier general.[1] CINCSPECOMME OPLAN 215-58 had no provisions for a joint ground force command, although both the respective Army and Marine planners understood that their forces could be employed under five of the eight courses of action discussed in the plan. The three remaining courses of action involved combined operations with the British. Probably because of a lack of guidance, the USAREUR planners of EP 201 established the organization shown in figure 8. The commander of the service with the most forces would act as the senior overall commander.[2]

The two ground force commanders reported to different higher headquarters: the Army to Commander, U.S. Army Forces, SPECOMME, and the Marines to Commander, U.S. Naval Forces, SPECOMME. Therefore, it was unclear who commanded the ground forces, and participants quickly realized that these units would have to coordinate their activities.[3]

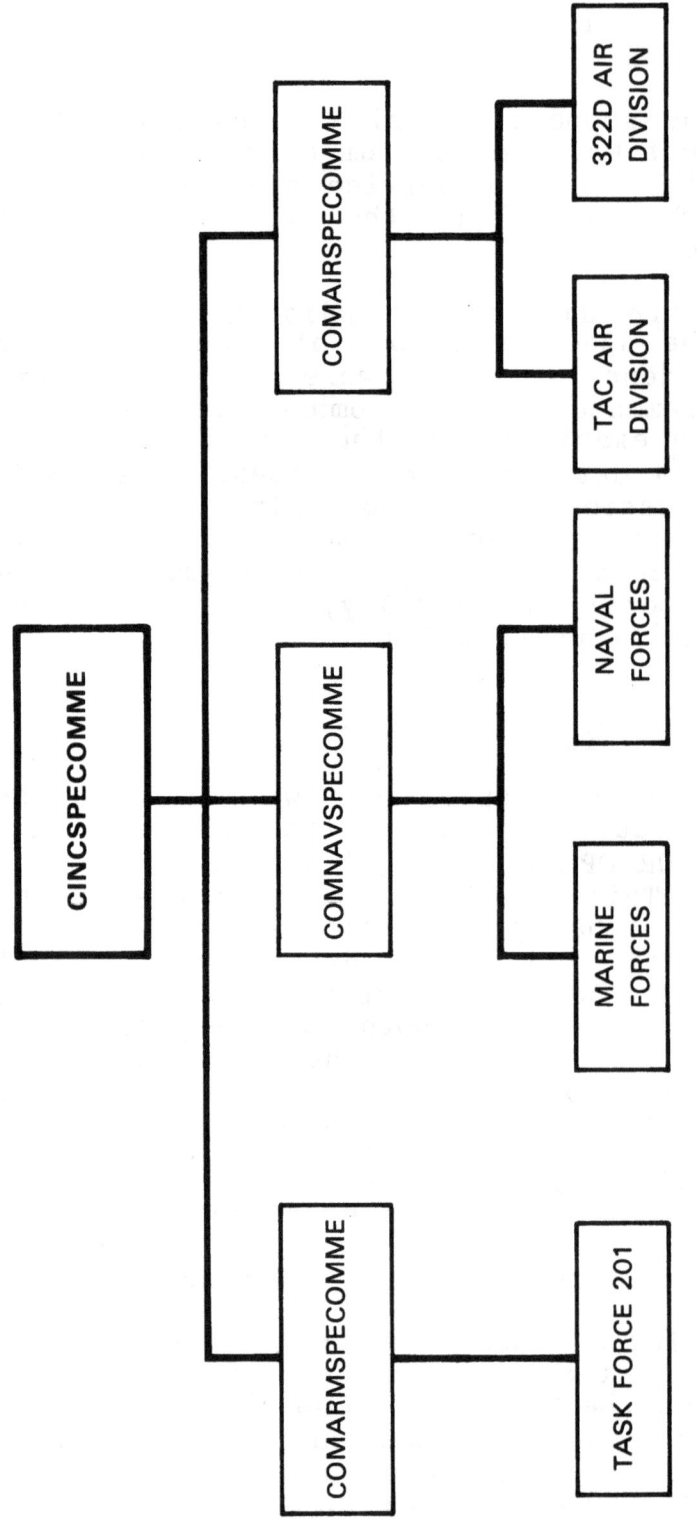

Source: "Infantry Conference Report," Comments, 211.

Figure 8. Organization for Operations

General Gray recalled that coordination between the Army and Marine Corps was good and that they accomplished their missions. The noncombat situation, however, provided the breathing space to establish a unified ground command. As General Gray described it: "More and more of my time was being spent coordinating with CINCSPECOMME, General Wade (the Marine ground commander), Admiral Yeager (Naval commander), Ambassador McClintock and the Lebanese. It was becoming apparent to me that most of that coordination could better be done at a higher level than my own."[4]

CINCSPECOMME recognized the accuracy of Gray's observation and created another headquarters, one for which planners had not foreseen a need.

CINCSPECOMME considered three solutions to increase coordination between the services. First, the senior brigadier general would become Commander, American Land Forces (COMAMLANFOR); second, CINCSPECOMME would coordinate the ground operations; and, third, a separate senior ground force commander would be appointed by the president.[5] CINCSPECOMME rejected the first course of action because both commanders were fully occupied commanding their own organizations and subsequent operations might have required the geographic separation of the two forces, further complicating command and control. CINCSPECOMME considered direct coordination inadvisable because such action would have made him, in effect, one of his own component commanders. Therefore, the establishment of a separate senior ground force command was the only realistic solution.[6] (See figure 9.)

On 21 July, CINCSPECOMME requested the Chief of Naval Operations, as executive agent for the President, to assign an Army or Marine major general or lieutenant general as COMAMLANFOR. On 23 July, DA, as directed by the JCS, designated Maj. Gen. Paul D. Adams for this assignment. As early as 15 July, General Adams had commented to General Gray that he might be sent to Lebanon to take command of all land forces.[7] Thus, Adams had about a week to prepare for his new assignment. But he stated later, "I was a little suprised that I didn't have any kind of definitive orders. . . ."[8] General Gray, however, endorsed the decision:

> We probably would have muddled through without the new command structure but might well have made some mistakes that need not have been made. General Adams gave firm direction to the entire operation and played a pivotal part in the many

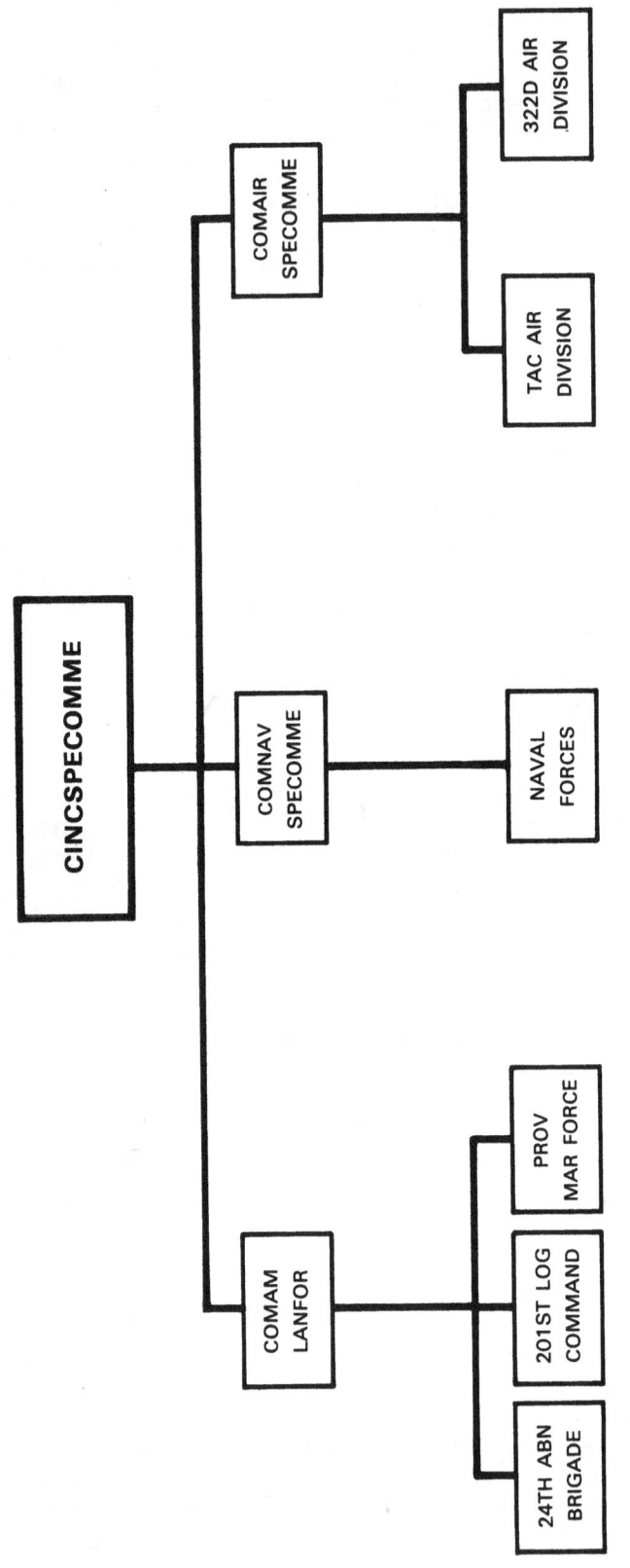

Source: "Infantry Conference Report," Comments, 226.

Figure 9. Organization for Operations (Final)

46

actions which were never publicized but which eventually nudged the Lebanese into burying their firearms for awhile and allowing the US to retract its forces.[9]

General Adams's first priority was to translate the broad mission directive into an operational mission statement. The overall goal was twofold: protect American lives and interests in Lebanon and sustain the independence of Lebanon. Adams identified the following specific tasks required to accomplish his mission:

- Maintain security around selected points such as the U.S. embassy, the Lebanese presidential palace, and the U.S. military base at the Beirut International Airport.

- Keep all principal routes of communications in and around Beirut and to the international airport and port area open and secure by frequent patrolling and by placing strongpoints along the routes.

- Secure Beirut from rebel invasion.

- Order frequent aerial reconnaissance missions over Lebanon and detailed aerial surveillance of routes leading into Beirut and routes leading from the Syrian border.

- Maintain a general reserve composed of two echelons: an immediate reserve of one airborne company and one tank company on the edge of Beirut along the airport road and a follow-on reserve of battalion strength supported by artillery and tanks.[10]

To accomplish these tasks, General Adams organized his forces as depicted in figure 10. The combat forces, the airborne brigade and the Marines, divided the specific ground tasks. Adams placed the 201st Logistical Command on an equal footing with the combat commands it supported.

Based on General Adams's guidance, Colonel Meetze determined that his mission was "to exercise command of the Army Supply and Service troops, ATF 201; to provide logistical support of all army troops in Lebanon; and to accomplish other missions that may be directed by CG, American Land Forces."[11] Specifically, the support command was to:

- Exercise command over all logistical troops assigned to ATF 201.

- Plan and conduct support operations with Army support forces assigned.

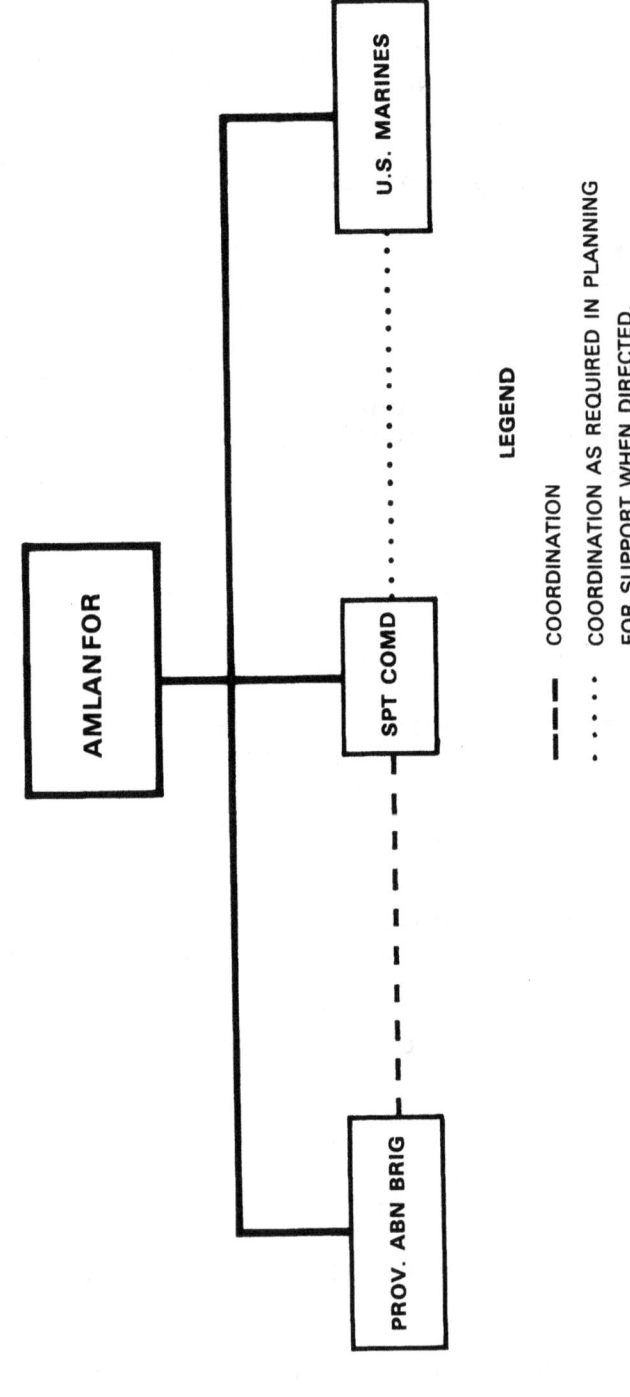

Source: 201st LC, "Report," including "Letter of Instruction," 30 July 1958.

Figure 10. Land Force Organization

● Conduct liaison with local Lebanese Army elements through the commanding general of the U.S. airborne brigade (all other liaison was required to go through AMLANFOR headquarters).

● Achieve a full support capability as rapidly as possible and provide local security of support installations and activities in coordination with the airborne brigade.

● Plan and conduct training of support personnel as necessary for operational support requirements.

● Receive and quarter incoming technical and administrative troops and coordinate security with the airborne brigade.[12]

Furthermore, Colonel Meetze subdivided these logistical missions into fifteen discrete functions:

● Procure, receive, store, maintain, and distribute supplies and equipment.

● Manage transportation service.

● Operate facilities for essential military operations, especially for the maintenance and repair of equipment, roads, railroads, and buildings.

● Provide medical care, including evacuation and hospitalization of the sick and wounded.

● Train troop units and individuals assigned or attached to the 201st Logistical Command.

● Control traffic within the assigned area.

● Procure necessary real estate.

● Provide rest camps, leave facilities, and welfare and recreational programs and facilities.

● Provide chaplain service.

● Operate the Army exchange service.

● Operate the Army postal service.

● Handle legal claims and judicial services.

● Handle finance and accounting services.

• Provide rear area defense and area damage control within the 201st Logistical Command area.

• Conduct civil affairs.[13]

Colonel Meetze organized the logistical command staff to command, control, coordinate, and direct the administrative and logistical support operations performed by its subordinate units (figure 11). The commander had a deputy commander, a directorate staff, a technical staff, and the normal administrative staff to assist him in discharging his responsibilities. The directorate staff had six sections, each charged with distinct staff responsibility in one of the following areas: personnel, security, plans and operations, supply and services, procurement, and civil affairs. The special staff had the normal administrative and technical responsibilities associated with its titles. In addition, it exercised "operational control of service units of [its] respective services."[14]

The 1957-58 curriculum of the Command and General Staff College at Fort Leavenworth, Kansas, taught officers to organize a primary staff for the logistical command. Possibly because of the enlarged responsibility and span of control, the primary staff officers were designated as directors. These directors had the general functions of assisting and advising the commander and deputy commander; formulating policies, plans, and directives; and coordinating and supervising the execution and implementation of plans by subordinate commanders.[15] Interestingly, the 1959 Field Manual 54-1, <u>The Logistical Command</u>, contained an organization similar to the one used in Lebanon in 1958 that specified directors instead of a primary staff. Evidently, those Army officers responsible for teaching and writing at the Command and General Staff College and those in field operations did communicate with each other. The result was a field manual based, in part, on practical experience.

The actual staff organization, however, did not match any pre-1959 field manual. It did follow a basic doctrinal tenet--that the organization should be flexible to support the operational mission. The former deputy commander of the 201st Logistical Command, Col. Dan K. Dukes, commented that "the entire organization and operation was a series and conglomeration of changes to the extent that if there was an original it could hardly be recognized."[16] This statement can be taken either as a positive reflection of a flexible doctrine or as a reaction to an operational problem without regard to

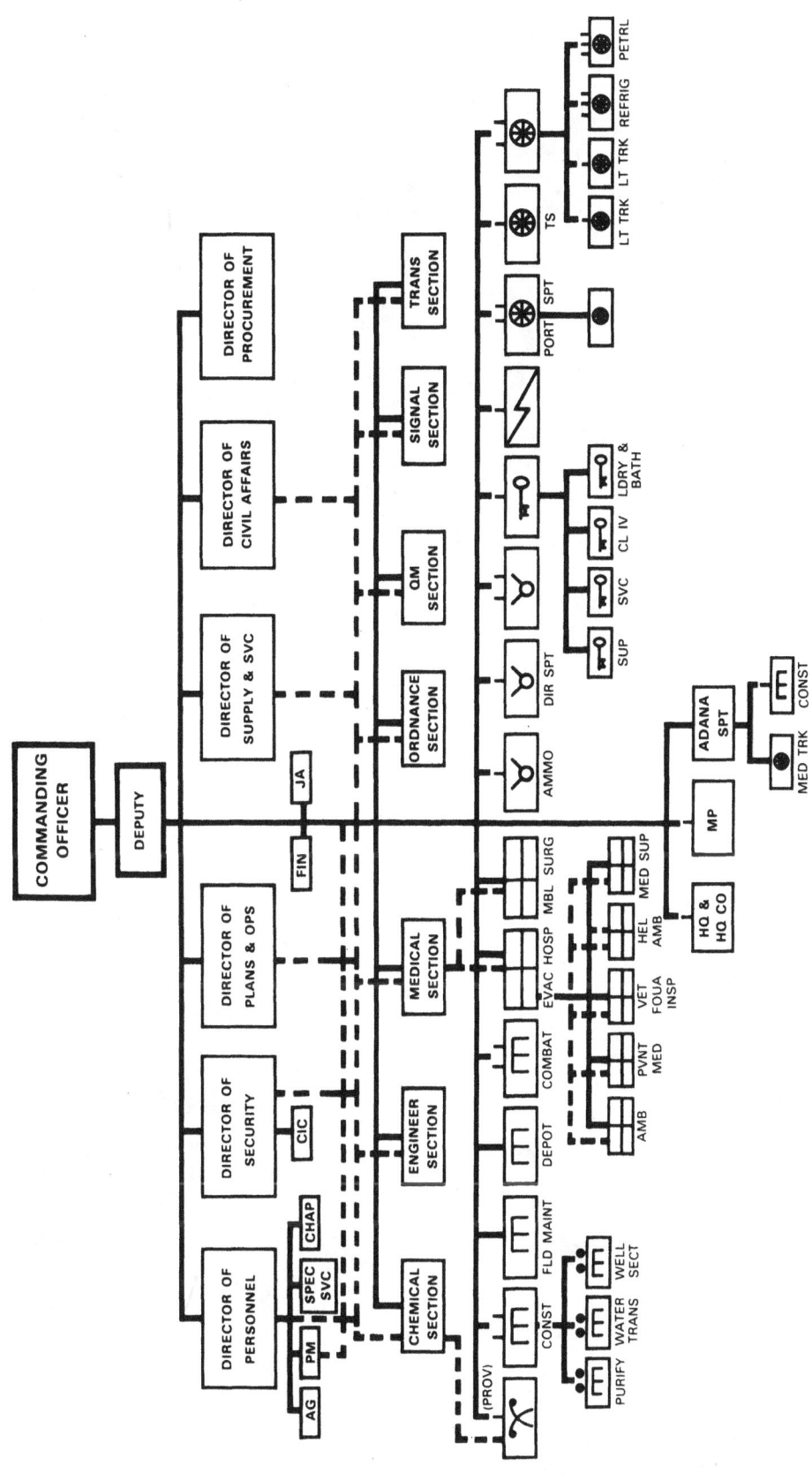

Source: Meetze, Papers Dealing with the Lebanon Intervention, Combat Studies Institute, U.S. Army Command and General Staff College, Fort Leavenworth, KS.

Figure 11. Organization of the 201st Logistical Command (A)

201st Logistical Command flag

Headquarters, 201st Logistical Command, Beirut, Lebanon, 1958

doctrine. In sum, it appears that existing field manuals did not greatly influence the organizational process.

A major change during the operation was the addition of an Adana, Turkey, support group, adding even greater numbers to an already large support force. Requirements to handle the supply storage and issue at Adana Air Base justified creation of the group because there was no permanent organization to manage a de facto pre-positioned storage site.

A primary purpose for the creation of the 201st Logistical Command was to have a single point of contact for all logistical matters. It succeeded in that purpose. The absence of combat contributed to the size and showmanship of the logistical effort. The G4/S4 of the airborne brigade and AMLANFOR headquarters, lacking serious operational planning duties, became more involved in the daily logistical operations by requesting data for briefing charts. The creation of AMLANFOR headquarters had a minimal effect on logistical operations except to add one more person to the briefings and statistical distribution lists. Coordination between the staffs was not a problem because sufficient time existed to accomplish this coordination through meetings and unhurried conversations.

The 201st Logistical Command experienced a few problems in its internal operation. Colonel Meetze's greatest difficulty was melding the command's approximately fifty separate military units and teams into a close, cohesive, functioning command. His task was all the more demanding because none of these units or teams had ever served, worked, or trained together as a team.[17] His deputy, Colonel Dukes, added this important postscript to the operation: "By the time Lebanon was all over, this conglomeration was just beginning to be sorted out and identified and able to function. . . ."[18]

Critics have charged that this command was too large. However, if the planned numbers of combat troops had actually been deployed to Lebanon for combat operations, a logistical organization of this magnitude would have been necessary to support the combat troops. Because there were no combat operations, the command appeared, in retrospect, to have been too large for the forces it supported. But it would have been foolhardy to plan a deployment without considering the risks and logistical requirements of combat. The support force turned its efforts from basic resupply to making life comfortable for the task force--better for the troops to be blessed with abundance than to suffer deprivation because of unforeseen circumstances.

The major difference between adequate plans and actual operations lay in the teamwork and practical operational procedures that naturally develop in realistic training exercises. The 201st Logistical Command was well planned and did provide one point of contact for all logistical operations. It was not, however, a smooth-running command until several months after deployment. It sufficed in Lebanon in 1958, but, to sustain a wartime deployment, combat service support elements need realistic training and exercises in peacetime. Such training instills teamwork and assures adequate, timely materiel support. Just as infantry units train as a team to assure battlefield success, so must support elements train together to ensure that battlefield success can be sustained.

Resupply

In Lebanon we unloaded mountains of supplies and equipment even after it was known there was no enemy; no fighting. This created problems and lost flexibility, gained nothing, indeed created a liability that could have caused great trouble and loss of life.19

Logistical doctrine requiring that X-days of supply* be on hand at any given time was the reason these "mountains" of supplies were delivered. They had been preordered and were automatically shipped in bulk to Lebanon from both USAREUR and CONUS.

Planning

Three factors governed logistical support planning for ATF 201: the requirement to deploy two battle groups, the necessity for rapid deployment, and the availability of aircraft. Annex D of EP 201 divided the logistical responsibilities, stipulating that USAREUR would be responsible for all logistical support of ATF 201 until either E+30 days or E+45 days if STRAC deployed, at which time DA would assume the task. USAREUR would furnish Alfa

---

*A day of supply was a unit used in estimating the average expenditure of various items of supply, usually expressed in pounds per man per day and in quantities of specific items.

and Bravo forces with the minimum basic supplies required to maintain combat operations until routine stateside resupply was established. Directly behind the deployed forces, airlift would carry the initial resupply and arrive in the staging area about E+3 days. This resupply would establish an initial level of about ten days' supply of class I and five days of class III, with additional air resupply ultimately increasing levels to about fifteen days of class I and ten days of class III. After setting these initial priorities, the plan stated that, in order to reduce the airlift requirements and increase troop deployment rates, all logistics would be on an extremely austere basis. Air logistical support was to be the minimum necessary to sustain operations and any unforeseen contingencies.

Normal supply buildup as dictated by the contemporary doctrine and overall logistical support would begin with arrival of sea resupply from both the USAREUR COMMZ and CONUS. USAREUR COMMZ would ship the initial resupply for the entire ATF, which would arrive at Iskenderun, Turkey, around E+20 days. This convoy would contain twenty days of all classes of supply. If required, emergency sea resupply from SETAF, then stationed in Italy, would arrive at about E+10 days and increase the buildup to twenty-five days of class I and twenty days of class III. EP 201 further charged SETAF to send an additional three basic loads of class V by E+10 days. Classes II and IV would be provided at the minimum to sustain operations; planners considered rationing class III in the early stages a distinct possibility.

The plan also directed USAREUR to support Charlie Force initially. If Charlie Force deployed by air, USAREUR was to provide enough supplies to sustain the force until arrival of sea resupply, about E+20 days. Delta and Echo forces deploying by sea would carry accompanying resupply in their transports to sustain them for about twenty days.

DA would ship an additional twenty days of all classes of supply to arrive at Beirut around E+30 days.[20] Those shipments from stateside would raise available supply levels from ten to thirty days. In addition, CONUS depots would continue automatic resupply with convoys, which contained supply for twenty days, arriving at twenty-day intervals in order to maintain a supply level of thirty days. The Army restricted the CONUS convoys to classes I, III, and V, with only limited quantities of classes II and IV and repair parts. Routine resupply would be operational after E+6 months.

55

Execution

On implementation of the plan, supply operators crated supplies stored in USAREUR. As noted earlier, supplies were not earmarked in Europe, so, although these supply workers found the supplies, the loading was haphazard. They loaded the first two scheduled COMMZ shipments (twenty days of resupply) on time and sealifted them from Saint-Nazaire and La Pallice to Beirut and to Iskenderun for transshipment to Adana, Turkey.21

Colonel Meetze later recalled that all went well until

> the arrival of the COMMZ first sea resupply shipment; identity of stocks as to shipment was lost. . . . This required many days to inventory and completely smothered the Quartermaster in receiving and documenting Class I supplies. I remember well the gracious gesture by General Gray, ATF 201, in loaning us a few men who worked around the clock with the Logistical Command personnel to make some semblance of order from piles of jumbled stocks.22

As noted in chapter 1, stateside resupply had already begun. In fact, because of a readiness exercise in June 1958, a month before the Lebanese crisis, most of increment one had already reached the U.S. ports. Following EP 201, DCSLOG released increment two for shipment to the ports and issued orders for depots to pick, pack, and hold increment three supplies. The total CONUS resupply was originally to consist of eleven increments, but developments in Lebanon soon made such massive resupply unnecessary, and only increment one was completely shipped. These supplies, a total of approximately 13,000 measurement tons, were loaded aboard three vessels at New York, Sunny Point, and Charleston. The vessels departed on 8 August. Because of lower than expected consumption rates, the troops in Lebanon did not require the class III and V supplies of increment two. Only the class I portion of this increment finally went forward. At New York, 900 measurement tons were loaded aboard Dalton Victory. Then, before the ship departed for Beirut on 25 August, it was further loaded at Hampton Roads with 1,100 measurement tons for the Marine Corps.23

The sealift cargoes arrived on time. However, because of the absence of hostilities and because resupply rates were based on wartime consumption, a huge surplus of supplies accumulated. It soon became clear that the theater could directly handle the reduced requirements of the Army forces in Lebanon. On 19 August, USAREUR indicated that it was prepared to assume complete resupply responsibility after the second CONUS shipment, the portion of increment two that left the port on 25 August. Consequently, no further EP 201 resupply shipments were made from the United States.[24]

The readiness exercise that had begun on 17 June enabled supplies to arrive as scheduled because most of increment one was already at the port ready for loading by E-day, 15 July 1958. This might have caused the stateside resupply to arrive too soon, but that was not the case. It took until 8 August to load the vessels fully, and these ships arrived in Beirut approximately fourteen days later, or a total of thirty-eight days after E-day, eight days longer than the planning figure. Starting from the time the readiness exercise began in June--and assuming the exercise was a full-scale effort--it took sixty-seven days for the resupply shipment to arrive in Beirut-- thirty-seven days over the planning figure! Thus, under the worst possible circumstances, ATF 201 would have had to rely on an emergency resupply effort for twenty-seven days, an unenviable position to be in. In short, if resupply had started from scratch, the logistical plan would not have been sufficient. Even under the artificially favorable circumstances of a readiness exercise, execution took eight days longer than planned. Obviously, the national supply system did not respond as fast as planners had envisioned.

The switch from CONUS to theater resupply was the first significant deviation from EP 201. Essentially, it was made to simplify the resupply effort and to turn off the stateside tap. According to Colonel Meetze, "Since only one battle group had been committed to Lebanon, and our situation did not reflect true combat conditions, our expenditure rates were found to be less for all classes of supply and timely action was necessary to reduce or divert automatic resupply to preclude large stock piles in the Beirut area."[25] The cancellation of the next nine and one-half increments from CONUS eased the stockpile situation in Lebanon but did not resolve the problem completely. Doctrine called for a specified amount of supplies to be available to deployed troops, so stockpiling was inevitable in an operational area.

Moreover, operational problems could have been avoided. Security considerations caused one difficulty. Another was the old curse of incomplete loading plans and cargo manifests. It was also apparent that the supply operators did not understand what constituted a basic day of supply. As the AMLANFOR after-action report made clear:

> The effectiveness of the Logistical Command in supply control function was hampered by the lack

of preparation of elements of the command for the operation. The supply personnel of the command did not know what items, in what amounts should be available for a day of supply for ATF 201 nor did they know the basis on which automatic supply was sent to the command from COMZ. The personnel of these teams by and large came from sources which depend on centralized supply control. They were not informed in advance of their role in EP 201 for security reasons, therefore, they did not have the official publication to compute days of supply at combat rates or to reconcile any rates they knew about with the quantities received in the automatic resupply shipment.[26]

Entire cargoes, most without manifests, were unloaded, inventoried, and temporarily stored, which caused further delay in the distribution and final storage of supplies. The delay was not critical (although it might have been disastrous had hostilities occurred). The most difficult cargoes were bulk loads. On 7 August, for example, one bulk load of forty commercial vans of class I supplies reached the quartermaster supply point at Beirut. These vans contained mixed loads of different types of rations (five-in-one, B, and C). The conditions of the loads and quantities of trucks made selective off-loading impossible. Soldiers unloaded the trucks' cargo in big piles. Hundreds of cases and domestic packs were broken, and loose items were scattered around the trucks. Shipside unloading caused most of the damage. Besides the immediate losses, it took time to organize all the loose items, inspect the damaged packages, and then properly distribute the rations to the field.[27]

Repair parts also arrived, for the most part, in bulk. In addition to confusion caused by incomplete manifests and bulk loads, the engineers, ordnance, and quartermaster personnel lacked technical manuals to identify properly these repair parts. These specialists were so busy trying to find what was available that, when a demand for a part arose, if they could even find it, they issued the part without proper accounting procedures. In fact, they never did develop the necessary supply planning.[28]

Once supply planners determined the days of supply,* reducing levels from thirty days to fifteen,[29] the

---

*In mid-September, the status of days of supply computation began to be based on the actual troop strength in Beirut.

COMAMLANFOR approved a plan that allowed for the selective discharge of cargo,[30] or taking only necessary items out of the ships and leaving the remaining cargo aboard. In that process, inaccurate or missing manifests made the task even more difficult. "[Because of] the lack of proper manifesting of vessels and because selective discharge was not contemplated at point of origin many items had to be off-loaded then back-loaded after required items [were] discharged."[31] This was a process not unlike unloading a full automobile trunk to get to a jack and then reloading the trunk.

Other unforeseen factors influenced the amount of materiel on hand, such as the local availability of petroleum products. Logistical planners, however, were unaware of this because the intelligence officers evidently did not route their estimates through the logisticians. With the amounts of materiel and petroleum products far in excess of that needed already in the resupply pipeline, more than selective discharge had to be done to avoid further port congestion. Staff officers had to divert supplies to Europe or to the Adana subcommand.

The importance of the base at Adana became readily apparent when the operational area, Beirut, began to bulge at the seams. Adana was therefore established as a prestockage point for the operation. "The mission of the subcommand as received from the 201st Logistical Command was to receive cargo from the port of Iskenderun, transport it to Incirlik Air Base, and establish a depot storage area for, at that time, approximately 15,000 tons of all classes of cargo."[32] Adana would maintain ten days of classes I, III, and IV and twenty days of classes II and V so the originally planned stockage would be available in the same part of the world.[33] As with supplies arriving in Beirut, Adana had problems with supply planning, particularly the acquisition of adequate storage areas, because of "a lack of firm information relative to the quantity and type of supplies to be received at Adana."[34] Confused procedures for diverting incoming ships to Adana caused added complications. AMLANFOR headquarters reported that "actions to accomplish adjustment in resupply were complicated by the need to make requests for diversions of CONUS shipments through several agencies, such as Department of the Army, the Overseas Supply Agency, N.Y., USACOMZEUR and CINCUSAREUR."[35]

Despite the problems, supply bundles accumulated in Beirut and Adana in sufficient numbers to meet the required days of supplies. (See appendix D for examples of on-hand supplies.) Except for class I (rations), the supplies generally remained in storage areas. Critics of the operation strongly recommended that a centralized on-call supply system would have been more efficient than automatic resupply. Although the automatic resupply satisfactorily met supply needs, a more efficient system for making a transition to an on-call resupply arrangement was needed for contingency operations.[36] With the noncombat situation in Beirut, the supply operators found it difficult to stop the incoming materiel because of the inflexibility of the automatic resupply system. As an after-action report stated: "Some energetic thought must be given to ways of adopting logistical support for STRAC type forces by providing fast dependable transportation and smaller increments of balance resupply rather than the 15 to 30 day ones used for this operation."[37]

The transportation of these supplies from the storage points to units did not present a problem once transportation companies arrived about two weeks into the operation. Until that time, combat troops used their own transportation. The static situation allowed the logistical command to consolidate all transportation operations under the 38th Transportation Battalion.[38] That battalion had adequate time to organize for its mission because it did not have to support a fast-moving, fluid situation requiring immediate attention. One might speculate on whether this battalion could have handled combat resupply, but, given the assets shown in the organization chart (figure 11), the transportation battalion would have done the job once ashore. If combat units had lacked organic truck transportation, there might have been problems because the majority of the transportation assets arrived too late in the operation to be of any use. In case of armed opposition after landing, the combat troops would have required the transportation battalion earlier, and it probably should have had a higher landing priority regardless. As the operation slowly unfolded, transportation was adequate. The central problem remained the unraveling of resupplies on the ground.

Colonel Dukes, in charge of supervising the resupply operation, recommended: "Where possible, and Lebanon is a good example, a water borne base should be used, facilitating a very gradual build-up on land only as conditions warranted and required it. I refer to a stream concept, vis-a-vis, the old line of so many days of supply ASAP and on the ground in the forward position."[39] Dukes makes a good argument for just-in-time logistics, water-borne, prestockage points, and a push-pull system of prepackaged bundles of resupply.

In Lebanon, the doctrine of maintaining X-days of supply on the ground was inefficient. Doctrine caused the diversion of combat troops from other duties to help unload unnecessary or redundant supplies. The resulting stockpiles offered a lucrative target and encouraged waste; for example, sixteen tons of Marine and ten tons of Army ammunition were dumped at sea due to damage in storage.40

Procurement

Under normal combat conditions, indigenous facilities, services and supplies would be obtained by seizure; however, in the Lebanon situation this was not practicable because of JCS directives relating to minimum interference with normal activities of the host nation.41

As the U.S. armed intervention in Lebanon lengthened, a predicament developed. Instead of a fast-moving assault operation, a large U.S. peacekeeping force staged a show of force in cooperation with the local government. Furthermore, the situation did not require the task force to live under combat conditions for extended periods. As a result, consumption of combat supplies remained below anticipated levels (although such supplies remained plentiful because of the automatic resupply system), while demand for other services soared. Normally, assault troops would have seized these other services, facilities, and supplies during the course of combat operations, but, since ATF 201 was cooperating closely with the Lebanese government, confiscation could not be considered. Instead, the U.S. government had to arrange for and buy supplies and services to maintain the image as an invited guest. Thus, an additional, unplanned procurement burden arose when obtaining supplies earmarked for troop welfare and adequate headquarters facilities. Specifically, the Army does not content itself to live on C-rations for months when other options exist. Even though piles of combat supplies were available, the task force undertook a large local procurement operation without adequate planning.

In the 201st Logistical Command, EP 201 established a procurement staff section of two officers and two enlisted men, plus a one-man procurement policy office in the Directorate of Supplies and Services to coordinate procurement policies.42 One officer of this procurement section arrived in Beirut on 20 July. He had no supplies or equipment of any kind. Thus, no procurement forms, regulations, or other directives were available. He did not know what fiscal appropriations existed, and, of course, no fiscal officer was available to provide fund certification.43 The primary cause of his predicament was operational security. The director of procurement for the 201st Logistical Command said later: "Guarding of the details, meaning, and objective of the plan must naturally be effected. However, in the recent operation, security was exercised to the point that the great majority of participants in key positions were not informed."44 Conceivably, he could have been referring to this particular officer or himself, or both.

The procurement officer, immediately on arrival, was verbally appointed as a contracting officer by Colonel Meetze, who instructed him to obtain locally those items needed to support the AMLANFOR ashore.45 Items procured included:

• Quartermaster--paper, pencils, stencils, and other expendable supplies; fresh fruits and vegetables for troop messes; coffee, brooms, maps, soaps, ice, and embalming service.

• Engineer--lumber, nails, plywood, hinges, crushed rock, paint, D-4 dozer parts, and use of bucket crane with operator.

• Medical--items required for use by the field hospital in patient treatment, laborarory services performed by the U.S. hospital in Beirut, and drugs.

• Transportation--stevedoring, bus transportation, and rail and truck transportation.

• Miscellaneous--minor signal, ordnance, and chemical items.46

How one man without supporting materiel was supposed to accomplish this task was not clear. Only the assistance of the U.S. embassy made the officer's job possible. The procurement officer immediately used the embassy to help contact Lebanese vendors. On 22 July, the embassy set up a liaison procurement section to contact and receive applications from local vendors and to deal with specified sources of supply. The embassy provided interpreters who overcame the formidable language barrier, and the system worked. The contracting officer made his needs known to the embassy. A liaison officer would then contact a local merchant and conclude a verbal agreement on price, quantity, and delivery. Verbal agreements were necessary because of the urgency of the demand and due to the lack of requisition forms and procurement personnel. The embassy provided limited typing assistance for ten or twelve purchase orders but could not cite funds because the appropriation data was unknown. The U.S. government found itself obligated, in most instances, by verbal contract, even to include requisition of real estate and property for use by the task force personnel.47 To pay for these items, the logistical command received $25,000 on 18 July and an additional $100,000 on 1 August from USAREUR.48

Evidently, the planners forgot to make provision for real estate procurement because no provision had been made to establish a real estate office. It was expected that these duties would be performed in the engineer staff section of Headquarters, 201st Logistical Command.49 Moreover, real estate transactions were a significant problem because "no one with procurement experience in the real estate field was included in any of the troop complements."50 The volatile political situation required quick action to find billets for the combat troops. This forced the contracting officer into verbal agreements with local landowners. Luckily, no major mistakes were made.

Water, which is of prime importance for military operations, particularly in the Middle East, was another immediate need. Each man had a five-gallon supply of water on the initial lift. Planners supposed that potable water could be obtained locally. Even with the cooperation of the local authorities, however, considerable effort was needed to acquire adequate supplies for the U.S. troops. No lakes or springs were in the area of operations, and the streams were bone dry. The city distribution system had branch lines that skirted most of the bivouac areas. However, Lebanese authorities rationed this supply, and peak demands for military use would have overtaxed the antiquated system. Also, rebels had sabotaged three distribution mains and associated branch lines. Consequently, wells were the only reliable source of water. Although the wells were numerous, access to them was poor and most had a small yield. Furthermore, while most well owners agreed to sell water to the U.S. Army, they insisted on reserving the right to use their well for six to eight hours each day for irrigation. Only a few wells produced a reliable yield on a twenty-four hour basis. Eventually, one well supplied 75 percent of the water for the command. The average consumption reached about nine gallons per capita per day for all purposes, including laundry service, showers, and road sprinkling. Civilian contractors offered to drill wells for the Army, but no contracts were let.51

The organization of the 201st included well-digging teams, but the need to procure land and the availability of other wells probably precluded activation of these teams. In a secured area, these teams could have eventually provided necessary water. But in a fighting situation, the unexpected difficulty in obtaining water might have caused serious problems. Greater attention should have been given to the procurement of water; merely assigning well-digging teams to the force was not sufficient.

Other procurement shortages included shop, warehouse, and refrigeration storage, which became acute when the operation turned into a peacekeeping mission in conjunction with the automatic resupply procedures. In addition, the need to conduct fair and legal rental agreements contributed greatly to the lack of warehouse space.

The 201st Logistical Command found itself unprepared for the large procurement demands it faced as there was no procurement annex in the plans. The procurement officer recommended that, in the future, "such an annex should include instruction on the proper method of submission of purchase requests, funding requirements, procurement procedures (to include time required to effect procurement), and a listing of items which by law may not be procured under any circumstances and/or unless certain conditions exist."52

Even without planning, the procurement activities did succeed, largely because of the presence of the U.S. embassy. Moreover, enough time was available to rectify the procurement effort, and the established procurement office in theater (USAREUR) responded readily to requests for funds to compensate for local procurement activities in Beirut.

Civil Affairs

". . . establish a base in the large olive grove just east of the airport . . . matter of military necessity. Send the bills to the Ambassador."53 These few lines created yet another difficulty. "One of the most serious problems involving the civil affairs staff," according to Colonel Meetze, "was the harvesting of the Olive crop."54

The decision to laager ATF 201 in the olive grove southwest of Beirut was probably made on the basis of both space requirements and the tactical situation as then known by the commander. The decision, however, did not consider civil affairs implications. U.S. forces eventually occupied 20 percent of the largest olive grove in Lebanon. This one grove produced an annual revenue of around $100,000 that was vital to the local economy. To further complicate the problem, some 200 different people owned the trees. With proper troop discipline, the trees would not be damaged, for the groves contained existing roads and open spaces for tents. The tactical situation was static, so, with the approach of harvest time (September through February), pickers could have been allowed in the area with the proper security measures. However, the Lebanese women, the traditional olive harvesters, refused to enter the groves while U.S. troops were present. This impasse could have caused the loss of the crop and created a serious unemployment problem.[55] A simple, seemingly logical decision had turned into a social as well as an economic problem. The United States might have been stuck with a substantial bill.

Many Americans and Lebanese spent long hours finding a solution. Eventually, the U.S. Army, embassy, and local Lebanese mayors reached agreement. A joint team made an initial estimate of the olive crop's value and agreed to a final assessment upon departure. The team encouraged owners to harvest their crops because only if the owner made a reasonable effort to harvest his crop would a claim for damages be considered. For security purposes, the U.S. Army issued passes to harvesters whose names appeared on lists submitted by local mayors. Landowners did make claims, but, more important, it took many meetings, much time, formation of ad hoc committees, and extensive staff work by the U.S. embassy and civil affairs section to correct a serious problem created by a simple tactical decision (table 4).[56]

Table 4. Summary of Claims Paid

Claims	Monetary Amount	
	Lebanese Pounds	U.S. Dollars
Olive Grove (crop, tree, and soil claims)	702,036.00	222,868.57
Real Property	360,428.00	114,421.58
Vehicle Damage	7,015.00	2,226.98
Total	1,069,479.00	339,517.13

(Based on a 1958 conversion rate of 3.15 Lebanese pounds to 1 U.S. dollar.)

Source: 201st LC, "Report," 13 October 1958 to 30 November 1958, 6.

For contingency operations in support of friendly nations, civil affairs activities are obviously important. Tactical planners, however, tend to ignore civil affairs, believing it is one of those things that others will take care of. The logistician must pay particular attention to civil affairs, for his activities are directly affected by the availability of local real estate, labor, supply, transportation, and the need for security. Generally, logistical commands have had a civil affairs staff because civil affairs was considered a service. As such, civil affairs needs to be preplanned.

Civil affairs planning for the operation, at best, was limited and, at worst, nonexistent prior to deployment. The civil affairs annex to CINCSPECOMME OPLAN 215-58 was dated 11 September 1958, nearly two months after U.S. Army forces had landed and civil-military relations had become a problem.[57] The civil affairs annex for CINCAMBRITFOR OPLAN 1-58 (Bluebat) did delegate authority, fix responsibility, and establish certain detailed functional policies for administration of civil affairs. Overall political direction was to be issued in supplemental political directives by the concerned governments. USAREUR EP 201 of 18 February 1958 called for supplementing the headquarters of the logistical command with three civil affairs teams (headquarters, language, and labor teams), thus creating a civil affairs staff of five officers and eleven enlisted men.[58] A recurring comment in after-action reports about these plans was that commanders did not receive adequate policy guidance from higher headquarters.[59] The reason planning is difficult for contingency operations is that actual employment locations may not be identified and that the conditions of employment cannot be determined in advance.

Still, it is possible to design in advance an organizational structure to handle such problems. Regardless of the situation, qualified personnel can be trained, and the headquarters level of responsibility can be determined in advance. For the Lebanese operation, there was no predetermined responsibility; instead, it had to evolve. To ensure consistency with official U.S. government guidance, the American ambassador was responsible for all public relations activities regarding U.S. military operations in Lebanon. CINCSPECOMME (with the J3 as supervisor) was responsible for developing civil affairs agreements with the Lebanese government, a status of forces agreement, and liaison with the U.S. embassy on all matters relating to military policy consideration. On the other hand, the J4 for the COMAMLANFOR established and conducted civil affairs within the area of ground operations.[60]

The civil affairs staff designated in EP 201 for the logistical command began arriving in Lebanon on 20 July. For reasons not clear, "none of these teams were used as such and all except two officers and two enlisted men were reassigned to other than Civil Affairs duties." These two officers and two enlisted men formed the Directorate of Civil Affairs for the 201st Logistical Command, and even they had the additional duty of special service activities.61

It is doubtful that the four-man team could have handled a situation similar to the one in Lebanon if it had deployed to a nation that had no diplomatic ties with the United States. Through the U.S. embassy liaison office in Beirut, the State Department negotiated with the Lebanese government about contracts between U.S. forces and Lebanese civilians. "This [diplomatic] office proved extremely valuable to the military and assisted greatly in the accomplishment of the [military] mission."62 A Lebanese-American Civil Affairs Committee (eventually elevated to "commission" status) was established by U.S. embassy and Lebanese officials to set policy, carry out coordination, and monitor indigenous resources. "The committee met weekly and its activities were instrumental in avoiding unnecessary adverse publicity and lengthy negotiations."63 This committee worked with the civil affairs office and helped to identify such operational problems as violations of public security, claims, use of public domain, use of indigenous labor, community relations, procurement, and monitoring of local resources. The committee also developed data about the Lebanese government, population densities, political aspects of interest to the U.S. forces, and other information relating to military and governmental activities and plans.64

The civil affairs staff considered a variety of everyday socioeconomic activities. These included legal matters, such as the status of forces agreement and foreign claims, public safety, curfews, fire and sabotage prevention, and general disaster relief as well as police and military cooperation, control of vendors, labor and union liaison, public health, food and agriculture policies, property control, public transportation, civil information, and political affairs. The civil affairs office handled all of these activities a month after U.S. forces landed in Lebanon. The Americans developed policies as problems arose, and the ambassador or a State Department representative was available to set the policy. However, such may not always be the case.

After-action assessments deemed the civil affairs staff for the Lebanese operation inadequate. These reports strongly recommended that civil affairs annexes include guidance for the military commander and the ambassador. These annexes must detail procedures so that the commander may effectively carry out the military and political policies of the United States. "This guidance must also provide for the contingency that U.S. diplomatic representatives may not be available in the national area in question."[65] The after-action reports asserted that the civil affairs mission was successful only because the ambassador diverted nine foreign service officers from the Foreign Service Institute, Arabic Studies Center, to the embassy liaison office.[66]

Because U.S. forces were in Lebanon twenty-three days without a status of forces agreement, a legal officer qualified in international law was required to adjudicate claims and draft a status of forces agreement. Such an agreement was essential for defining the legal guidelines for U.S. military personnel in a host nation. Status of forces agreements normally include rights of criminal jurisdiction, freedom of U.S. military personnel from civil action, exemption of U.S. military forces from taxation, free entry into a sovereign nation without inspection, the right to implement appropriate security measures to protect U.S. forces, and freedom of movement by U.S. personnel. For a contingency operation, it obviously is difficult to prepare a status of forces agreement in advance. It is possible to prepare a draft agreement and execute it at a favorable moment, probably as close as possible to the time when a nation requests U.S. aid.[67] Therefore, civil affairs annexes must also have sufficient guidance (perhaps in the form of a model or draft outline) so that the commander can negotiate an agreement with the foreign governments if no U.S. diplomatic representatives are available.

The civil affairs officers in Lebanon understood that exact, detailed planning might not be possible in the future, but they raised several questions that tomorrow's planners must address:

1. Should claims be accepted from the foreign government when United States forces are present on an invitational basis? On a noninvitational basis?

2. Should payment of fees for services, use of public domain or facilities be entertained from the foreign government or its legal entities when forces are present on an invitational basis? On a noninvitational basis?

3. Should the United States consider the claims of the indigenous private citizen or should such claims be shifted to the foreign government?

4. Should the claims function rest with the military forces or with embassy officials? (In either case, staff augmentation will be required very early in the operation. If military, component commanders should be granted authority to appoint foreign claims commissions. This authority should be effective upon assumption of command.)

5. Is the use of private property and facilities limited to normal contract, lease and purchase-type agreement, or mutually acceptable free use?[68]

Finally, based on the Lebanese experience, civil affairs officers recommended that, when a foreign government invites U.S. troops to enter its nation, the sovereign government should make provisions for adequate bivouacs for troops. Because such laager space was not prearranged, the Lebanese government assumed that the U.S. forces would locate their own areas. This placed the U.S. commander in the embarrassing position of bargaining with individual Lebanese citizens who did not want to release their property to the Americans.[69] As a final comment, an after-action report warned that civil affairs succeeded only because, in the noncombat situation, commanders had time to devote to it and because the U.S. embassy provided excellent support.[70]

Medical Support

. . . majority of fleet medical officers . . . ashore were gynecologists, psychiatrists, and obstetricians. . . .[71]

It is a long established fact . . . that any force deployed overseas requires the full range of medical support on a continuing basis, regardless of the combat situation, because diseases and injuries are normal to all military operations.[72]

Medical support for U.S. personnel was left to the service commanders. CINCSPECOMME supervised, coordinated, and monitored supporting plans and operations of the service commanders, but CINCSPECOMME made each service responsible for providing medical support for its own forces in accordance with existing interservice agreements. The plan did not provide or reference specific medical planning information for, most significantly, local area health problems, prevalent area diseases, and local sanitation conditions. All of these factors might have had a debilitating effect on the health of U.S. forces.[73]

The Commander, U.S. Naval Forces, SPECOMME, was responsible for providing medical care for the amphibious troops while they were embarked with his command. The plan failed to specify which commander assumed this responsibility after the troops had landed. Surprisingly, at the CINCSPECOMME level, Army and Air Force medical personnel neither wrote nor reviewed the operational plan.[74]

Based on CINCSPECOMME's plan, each component (the Army, Air Force, or Navy) developed its own respective medical support plans, with little apparent coordination. The Army, for instance, did not even receive a copy of either the Air Force or Navy medical plan. Each service worked in isolation "without reference to the over-all medical needs of the operation."[75] The Army medical representatives were unaware of the overall medical service responsibilities until the operation had begun. Army planners did not interpret SPECOMME's plan to mean the Army had responsibility to support the Marines ashore. As the operation progressed, the Army did provide clearing company and evacuation hospital support as well as certain supply and other services for all forces ashore. This action stretched Army resources thin because planners had anticipated only the demands of Army troops.[76]

A lack of planning coordination forced each service to conduct an independent medical support program. There was no overall coordination or cooperation on supply operations, medical evacuation, or locations of medical support units. This oversight interrupted the flow of information concerning the medical organization within each service, proposed locations of field hospitals, and the extent of medical resources and support each service would provide.[77] For example, "while the Army and Navy were moving specially qualified personnel and units into the area, the Air Force was withdrawing personnel with these same skills. Supply shortages developed in one service necessitating extraordinary procurement action, while another service apparently had quantities of the needed items immediately available in the area."[78]

The Army eventually had adequate organic medical support. Surgical facilities and operating rooms aboard the SPECOMME commander's flagship were available, although only because of local coordination. When necessary, and not through planning, the American University Hospital in Beirut treated overflow cases. An evacuation hospital did not become operational until eight days after the alert, and resupply remained a serious problem.

Although medical supplies were adequate at first, the supply system did not respond readily to the medical needs that developed. "Medical resupply did not take into consideration specific items that were very 'fast moving' due to environmental conditions experienced."[79] Medics, however, used expedients, such as local procurement. The items in short supply were the common, but necessary, ones needed for treatment of diarrhea and heat exhaustion. Medical officers had difficulty requisitioning emergency medical items through the military supply system because medical supplies were integrated into the routine supply system along with all other items. Priorities already established within that supply system slowed responsiveness.[80] (In the 1950s, evidently to centralize the resupply system, medical items became part of the overall resupply system. Thus, a winch part could have had priority over a medical item. Medical resupply has since returned to medical channels.)

The medical supply system was also overburdened because, in April, USAREUR COMMZ ordered the Army to support all U.S. forces during an operation. The medical supply officer, however, did not learn of this added requirement until Delta Force, with the field hospital, had already arrived at the operational area in August. Then the logistical command informed the medical supply officer for the 58th Evacuation Hospital that he would issue medical supplies to all troop units within the task force and act as head of the force medical depot. This confusion and late notification resulted in a shortage of the medical supplies needed to perform the new added mission. Stocks of fast-moving items were depleted within a short time. While still in Germany, the medical supply officer tried to ascertain where medical supplies would be issued. Unable to do that, he assumed the Navy was in charge. As it turned out, the Navy did not have sufficient medical supplies available and even had to draw on Army stocks occasionally.[81]

Other problems abounded. The initial high security classification of the plans also affected the resupply effort. Even the twelve-man medical supply depot team "had no medical supplies nor information thereof"; the team never saw the classified plan and had no idea of what to do.[82] Some supplies were outdated; for example, the

71

plaster paper used in casts was dated 9 March 1944. The medical personnel were carried in one ship and their equipment in another, with the resultant confusion and loss of equipment after landing that was characteristic of other task force elements. A majority of the medical officers involved in the operation believed that "if casualties (combat) had been encountered, it would no doubt have been a medical calamity and many saveable lives would have been lost" because of the lack of surgical facilities ashore during the initial stage.[83] This is a valid conclusion and again illustrates that the lack of prior coordination and the unclear division of responsibility might have proved fatal to the task force if it had met determined resistance.

Security

Plans for the operational security of the airhead were drawn up by General Gray's staff the day before the airborne force left Adana for Beirut. These plans seemed as if they had been "lifted from the diagram in the field manual for defense of an airhead."[84] (See map 3.) General Gray wrote later:

> It would have disposed our troops in company-size strong points on the semicircular ridge of hills that rose to the south and east of the airport and the open sand dunes to the north with the ocean to the west. I believed that if we had trouble it would come from small forays or acts of individuals such as snipers, fanatics or thieves, and it would be better to initially, at least, dispose ourselves in a tight perimeter, largely in the olive grove east of the airport where we could protect ourselves by mutual support as well as provide a secure area for the support units that were to follow.[85]

To counter the threat preceived by General Gray, the forces built defenses based on the current mobile defense doctrine that located troops so they could be quickly assembled at rendezvous areas. Without enough men to stop all small-scale infiltration, Gray's staff officers based their plans on the capability of the Lebanese army and civilian agencies to acquire the necessary intelligence for them to assemble the requisite forces to counter an attack. The forces finally deployed in positions inside the area indicated by the broken line on map 3 with three rifle companies occupying forward ready positions. Some platoons within each company developed tactical positions; however, the majority of each company remained in an administrative bivouac ready for rapid movement. The

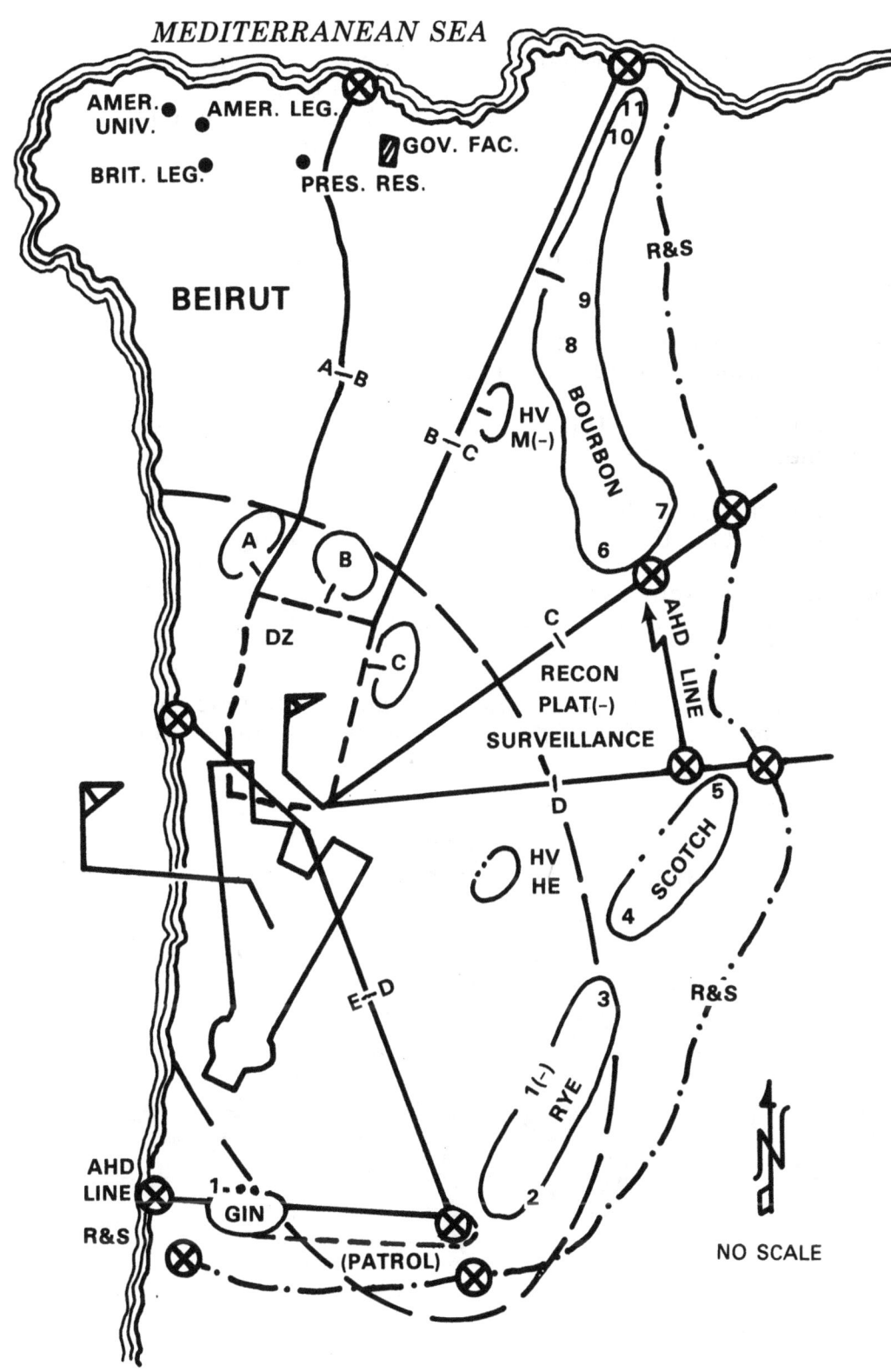

Source: "Infantry Conference Report," Comments, 227.

Map 3. Security Plan

brigade commander detailed one company as an airfield guard and kept one company in reserve in the olive grove to provide security for brigade troops, the support command, and the line of communication to Beirut. There were sixteen rendezvous areas located throughout the sector where troops could quickly move in case of an emergency.[86]

The airborne staff developed six contingency plans to handle these emergency situations:

● OPLAN Cover moved U.S. forces to block any entry of organized combat forces into Lebanon.

● OPLAN Extraction covered the withdrawal of U.S. troops when ordered.

● OPLAN Deep Freeze provided for winter dispositions in the event the U.S. occupation was prolonged.

● OPLAN Rescue implemented the rescue of key U.S. and Lebanese officials and family members from their offices or residences.

● OPLAN Shoforce called for the movement of tactical units in and around Beirut to impress continually on the

Brig. Gen. David W. Gray inspecting a guard post

dissident elements the U.S. presence and readiness to intervene.

• OPLAN Cyclone called for tank-infantry teams to move quickly to any locality in the city of Beirut to reduce roadblocks or establish tactical positions.[87] "These cyclone forces were used on quite a few occasions and were very effective in quieting the situation down, as neither side wished to get us involved. They were also effective in keeping our troops on their toes and thus assisted in the maintenance of high morale."[88]

The airborne force expected to conduct security operations and apparently had little difficulty in doing so. However, the logistical command was less flexible. After-action reports discussed the perennial conflict within technical units between operational effectiveness and physical security. As with many modern-day support units, ordnance, quartermaster, medical, transportation, and other units claimed that their operational effectiveness declined when they had to provide guard details. The ordnance units claimed a loss of 60 percent effectiveness due to guard requirements.[89] The support units probably assumed, as they do today, that "someone" would provide security so that mechanics could be mechanics, supply people could perform supply functions, ammunition handlers could care for ammunition, and so forth. The plans for the Lebanese operation, however, assumed that each support unit would protect itself and did not specify a separate security force to guard the bulging supply stocks that filled the area because of the automatic requisition system.

The logistical plan did provide for a Directorate of Security that was charged with typical security duties, including communications, plans, intelligence, and counterintelligence. On arrival in Beirut, though, this directorate discovered that it was unprepared for such duties: when those assigned to the directorate opened their sealed classified folders of maps and intelligence studies, they found the material was revelant only to Turkey.[90]

Initially, then, the Directorate of Security lacked information and current intelligence. Later, physical security for the mountains of supplies bedeviled this security office. Other security matters rested with the AMLANFOR headquarters and the airborne brigade. The director of security established liaison with the G2 of ATF 201, the Lebanese port security officer, the Lebanese railway maintenance officer to U.S. forces, and the Beirut

U.S. Army guard post in Lebanon

municipal police chief. The director of security insisted that tactical troops of the 187th Airborne Group perform guard duty. However, in a 12 September 1958 memorandum for record, General Adams told the logistical command that the supply personnel were responsible for the security of storage areas and that every unit was subject to the guard rosters. A 201st Logistical Command report stated that the major security problem since the arrival of technical service supplies and equipment was finding guard personnel. Because the logistical command had no organic guard unit, the technical service troops worked at their normal duties during daytime and stood guard duty at night. Numerous guards were needed to prevent pilferage or sabotage of supplies during unloading at the port area and airfield and during truck or rail transport to storage areas. Also, many guard posts were required to protect the open storage areas. The technical service personnel already had a heavy work load just to sustain the resupply effort. They worked abnormally long hours under primitive conditions, and their performance of both duties naturally suffered. These factors physically exhausted them to the point that their efficiency as guards was questionable.[91]

General Meetze later gave an example of the problem in his description of one pilferage incident:

Petty pilferage of Class I stocks in the olive grove at night by native Lebanese was always a problem. I remember quite well a security incident involving the Quartermaster Depot area in the olive grove. Trees were spaced roughly 10-20 feet apart and not an olive tree could be removed without the personal authority of commanders of AMLANFOR's subordinate elements. The QM Depot area in the olive grove was protected by six sections of concertina wire which encircled the entire storage area. Three sections were placed together . . . and separated by a path the width of a jeep which made periodic circles of the area at night. There were no lights in the area. One morning, the company commander of the provisional quartermaster company informed me that a circus tent, folded in sections, had been stolen the night before. How anyone, or even many persons, could get these huge pieces of canvas across six sections of concertina wire without arousing the sentry on duty or being observed by the jeep driver will never be known. . . .[92]

Nonetheless, whether they liked it or not, the service units had to provide their own security. This probably was fair, for combat units had specific missions and should not have been tied down on guard duty. To avoid unneccessary reduction in the efficiency of technical service units, planning must consider rear area security. Reserve brigades may be able to fulfill the large rear area security mission, but serious thought should be given to troop lists and service unit strength so that these units have adequate security and are capable of performing their mission.

CHAPTER 4

CONCLUSIONS

Retraction

AMLANFOR staff officers began planning for retraction of U.S. forces shortly after their arrival. The lessons learned in the initial load-out proved valuable as retraction proceeded smoothly. The units, especially the service units, now had practical experience in making loading plans and manifests for sea and air movements. By departure time, they had diverted unneeded supplies and finished the final inventory of supplies on the ground. The greatest benefit of the deployment was the application of lessons learned for a smooth retraction. Most important, the tactical and political environment enabled the unit to plan and implement a phased withdrawal.

The withdrawal went well because it was the entire command's sole task after October 1958. Headquarters, AMLANFOR, terminated operations on 20 October, and all except a small rear party of the 201st Logistical Command had departed by 24 October 1958.[1] The small rear party departed in November, and the 201st Logistical Command was formally deactivated on 14 November 1958.[2]

General Adams was determined to take all on-hand supplies back with the command. His men did this, with the exception of several tons of ammunition that had been dumped into the sea. The force could do this because the units had just completed a traumatic move and they had the time to inventory available supplies and to plan for their retrieval. Most U.S. units moved to Lebanon in less than a week, while the withdrawal took over thirty days. The lesson of the retraction operation is that all the units knew the plans and, thus, were better able to execute them without major snags.

Summary

General Adams's forces accomplished the overall mission in Lebanon. They followed existing contingency plans, and the U.S. Army demonstrated its ability to deploy rapidly. The operation also served as a practical test of an emerging logistical doctrine of tailoring support forces to a specific ground force mission. Furthermore, the planning process provided valuable lessons for future operations.

The tailoring of logistical forces worked, but not without drawbacks. The designated support units must have a working knowledge of the plans so that they can devise complementary plans. Support units, like combat units, must train together to ensure teamwork. Higher headquarters must integrate the nonorganic combat service support units into the planning process and ensure that those units have an opportunity to rehearse the aspects of plans that affect their operations.

Another critical aspect of the planning process is worst-case planning. Worst-case planning means forecasting the worst situations that a deployed force may encounter. Worst-case planning, in conjunction with a logistical doctrine of pushing supplies forward, might have led to the problems encountered in Lebanon during 1958 and to similar problems in the Dominican Republic during 1965. The after-action reports of the Dominican Republic operation read as if they applied to Lebanon. These reports stated that the automatic resupply procedures were not sufficiently flexible to cope with changing requirements. One of these after-action reports, Operation Debrief, declared that "all interviewees stated that to some degree the automatic resupply was wasteful, inadequate, uneconomical, and generally mixed up." Moreover, the procedures to change automatic resupply were inadequate or nonexistent. Similar conclusions were reached for the earlier Lebanon operation. Although the automatic resupply or push system (the buildup of supplies according to levels for X number of days) met requirements, it was labor intensive and did not readily adapt to changing situations. It also required secure, spacious areas for storage, particularly if units did not consume the supplies immediately. This system created waste and piles of unused supplies.

As mentioned earlier, these factors were caused by worst-case planning in conjunction with this particular logistical doctrine. In Lebanon, the lack of fighting (a best-case situation) freed manpower to handle massive resupply shipments. In this situation, worst-case planning did not balance the need for combat power against a labor-intensive logistical effort. If worst-case planning had come to fruition and heavy fighting had ensued, then the logistical effort would have been severely taxed. A dilemma develops in planning for heavy combat between the size of the fighting forces and that of follow-on support. Only by engaging in limited or no fighting would the manpower be freed to manage the logistical system. A solution is to combine the push-pull systems. Furthermore, such a system comes closest to the goal of just-in-time logistics.

The logistical doctrine used by the U.S. Army during the 1983 operation in Grenada was a combined push-pull system. Logistical personnel had prepackaged supplies designed for a Grenada-type contingency operation. The units that deployed to Grenada also preconfigured resupply packages. Generally, these supplies were sent to the operational area on request by the deployed unit, but an automatic system was also used for certain resupply (mainly ammunition) items. In this case, the system was flexible enough to change the packages based on actual requirements. In some instances, supply personnel on Grenada made requests for special items, which normally would have taken at least a day; yet, a few minutes after their request, a plane would land carrying the needed items. The logistical personnel had already anticipated that request, and these instances indicated the close working relationship between the deployed force and the logistical personnel. It may be years before full disclosure of the Grenada operation can be made, but, based on the Lebanese and Dominican Republic experiences, the combined push-pull system appears to be the best of both worlds.

The operational lessons of the Lebanese operation are as old as military art itself and are just as critical now as at any time in the past. The detailed execution of plans, such as the proper implementation of loading plans, and the meticulous marking of cargo manifests are crucial. Practice exercises and rehearsals are needed to ensure this capability. Unrealistic loading plans will disrupt the best-made plans for a strategic movement. Inattention to detail adds confusion in the objective area and belies efficient planning.

Planning for the deployment of the airborne battle group was, in the sense of mission accomplishment, effective. But there were significant omissions in joint and theater planning, particularly for the resupply of potable water and medical support and for civil affairs.

In planning for water resupply, well-digging teams were assigned to the force. Finding a potable water supply in Lebanon, even within a secure area and with local cooperation, proved difficult. In a hostile environment, it could have proved catastrophic. Even such solutions as providing off-shore water tankers or saltwater converters would have been vulnerable in a hostile environment.

The cooperation, coordination, and planning for medical support were inadequate. More must be done for future operations, for this is a fairly simple joint planning task. After the Lebanese operation, the Army again streamlined medical resupply and confirmed a need to keep medical resupply in medical channels.

Civil affairs and procurement activities were other areas in which planning failed. The plans did not provide adequate guidance to the commander, and, therefore, these activities were only accomplished through support provided by the U.S. embassy and the time available because of the nonhostile situation. Any future planning must seriously consider the civil-military arena.

Finally, at the unit level, the commander and staff officers involved in a deployment will inevitably encounter varying degrees of confusion and poor coordination. Once the unit is en route to the objective area, the commander will feel relieved, but many nagging questions will remain. Overclassification and rigid planning compartmentalization breed confusion. Therefore, the planner must balance security requirements with the units' need to know. Improperly disseminated plans not only promote confusion, but also occasion slovenly appearance and poor performance. The most important planning lesson from the Lebanese experience is that planners must use a classification commensurate with security requirements and not create a smug in-the-know elite. If security restrictions prevent units from learning their assigned roles in a mission, it is self-defeating.

Prior planning and rehearsal of the support function are equally important to the success of a mission. In the case of Lebanon, Grandios, the deployment rehearsal plan for the combat units, proved to be the U.S. forces' salvation. Equal consideration must be given to logistical units. Rehearsal also implies training, and training logistical units as a team must be accomplished.

APPENDIX A

PLANS

Swaggerstick: Unilateral U.S. Army plan for Middle Eastern contingency operations.

CINCSPECOMME 215-58: A plan prepared by the Commander in Chief, Specified Command, Middle East, for conducting various types of military operations in Middle East countries. Primary consideration was the military implications of the Eisenhower Doctrine for the Middle East.

CINCAMBRITFOR OPLAN 1-58 (Bluebat): A combined plan in which the U.S. portion was an adaptation of the plan for Lebanon contained in CINCSPECOMME 215-58. This was then coordinated with the British War Office for conducting a combined U.S.-U.K. operation. The JCS ordered that the U.S. portion of this plan be executed for the Lebanese operation.

USAREUR EP 201: A plan prepared by USAREUR in support of the CINCSPECOMME plan for Middle East operations.

24th Infantry Division EP 201: A plan prepared by the 24th Infantry Division in support of USAREUR EP 201.

Grandios: The 24th Infantry Division's load-out and marshaling plan in support of EP 201.

APPENDIX B

TASK FORCE 201

Alpha Force	Bravo Force	Charlie Force	Delta Force	Echo Force
1st Abn BG, 187th Inf	1st Abn BG, 503d Inf	TF HQ	HQ & ADM Tm, 85th Cml Bn	Tk Bn
LNO Arty Btry		Cbt Engr Bn	Sup Tm, 85th Cml Bn	
Engr Plt		A Btry, 13th FA Bn	Maint Tm, 85th Cml Bn	
Cbt Spt Plt		C Btry, 13th FA Bn	Unit Mess Tm, 85th Cml Bn	
Fwd Air Controller		AAA Btry	Fld Maint Tm, 581st Engr Co	
Cbt & Gp Flt HQ		Trp C (Recon), 2d Sqd, 9th Cav	Engr Const Bn, 79th Engr Bn	
TF Trp		E Co (Abn), 3d Engr Bn	2 Well Drill Tms, 7th Engr Bde	
TF Tac HQ		Det, 24th Avn Co	Pdn Plt, 687th Water Sup Co	
Prov Arty HQ		Det, 24th QM Co		
Clearing Plt		HHC, Log Comd A		
Advance Pty COMMZ				

Alpha Force	Bravo Force	Charlie Force	Delta Force	Echo Force
Det, 24th Sig Bn (Abn)		MP Co (-Plt), 382d MP Bn	Depot Sup Tm, USA Engr Dep	
		1 Co Engr Const, 79th Engr Bn	Army Surg Hosp, Hel Amb Tm, 47th Med Det	
		Evac Hosp (Semi-Mbl), 58th Evac Hosp	Prev Med Co (Sep) (-),485th Prev Med Co	
		1 Plt Amb Co, 30th Med Gp	Prev Med Sup Tm, USA Med Det	
		Dir Spt Co, 47th Ord Gp	Amb Co (-Plt), 30th Med Gp	
		Mag Plt, Ammo Co, 57th Ord Gp	Vet Food Insp Tm	
		Bath Plt (-), QM Gp	Ord EOD Tm, 85th EOD Det	
		Unit Mess Tm, 15th QM Bn	Bakery Plt (-), 134th QM Co	
		POL Sup Plt (-), 215th QM Bn	Co HQ Tm, 2d QM Gp	
		Sup Tm, QM Gp	Ldry Plt (-), 2d QM Gp	
		Aerial Sup Tm, 557th AS Co		

Alpha Force	Bravo Force	Charlie Force	Delta Force	Echo Force
		Stor & Iss Sec, 545th Sig Co	Unit Mess Tm, 15th QM Bn	
		Prov Det ASA (USASAE)	Mess Tm Aug, 2d QM Gp	
		1 Co, 533d Trk Co	Autmv Maint Tm (-), 2d QM Gp	
		Prov Port Supv Det, 11th Trans Bn	Autmv Maint Tm, 2d QM Gp	
			Labor Tm, 95th QM Gp	
			Plt HQ Tm, 2d QM Gp	
			POL Lab Tm (-), 2d QM Gp	
			GRREG Plt, 565th QM Co	
			Salv Tm, 2d QM Gp	
			Sig Spt Co (-), 160th Sig Spt Gp	
			Photo Tm, 97th Sig Bn	

Alpha Force	Bravo Force	Charlie Force	Delta Force	Echo Force
			Radio Rpr Tm, USA Sig Dep	
			Trans Trk Bn (HHC), 38th Trk Bn	
			Lt Trk Co (Aug), 82d Lt Trk Co	
			2d Lt Trk Co (ROCID) (Aug), 125th Trk Bn	
			Med Trk Plt (Refrig), 1st Trk Co	

APPENDIX C

PERSONNEL AND EQUIPMENT FOR ALPHA, BRAVO, AND CHARLIE FORCES

Alpha Force

Personnel		Equipment	
TF Troops	200	3/4-T Trk	18
		1 1/2-T Tlr*	3
TF Tac HQ	(80)	1/4-T Trk	57
Prov Arty HQ	(2)	2 1/2-T Trk*	3
Clearing Plt	(40)	1 1/2-T w/Tlr	5
Prcht Sup &		3/4-T Tlr	8
Maint Det	(26)	1/4-T Tlr	46
Adv Pty COMMZ	(4)	106 RCLR	16
Det, 24th Sig		H-13	1
Bn (Abn)	(48)	L-19	2
		Water Purif	2
Abn Cbt Tm	1,483	TOE Equip	
		Class I	
Abn BG	(1,425)	Class III	
LNO Arty Btry	(2)	Class V	
Engr Plt	(33)	Water	
Cbt Spt Plt	(13)	Delivery Equip	
Fwd Air		Total STON	470
Controller	(1)		
Cbt Gp Flt HQ	(9)		
Adv Pty, Abn BG	10		
(Bravo Force)			
	1,693 217 STON		

Recapitulation

Personnel	1,693	217 STON
Equipment		470 STON
	1,693	687 STON

*Airlanded

Bravo Force

Personnel		Equipment	
TF Trps	54	3/4-T Trk	10
		1/4-T Trk	41
TF Adv HQ	(43)	1 1/2-T w/Tlr	2
Prov Arty HQ	(6)	3/4-T Tlr	9
Adv Pty COMMZ	(5)	1/4-T Tlr	40
		106 RCLR	16
Abn Cbt Tm	1,483	H-13	1
		L-19	2
Abn BG	(1,425)	TOE Equip	
LNO Arty Btry	(2)	Class I	
Engr Plt	(33)	Class III	
Cbt Spt Plt	(13)	Class V	
Cbt Gp Flt HQ	(9)	Water	
Fwd Air		Delivery Equip	
Controller	(1)	Total STON	384
	1,537 201 STON		

Recapitulation

Personnel	1,537	201 STON
Equipment		394 STON
	1,537	595 STON

Charlie Force

	Number	Weight
Aerial Sup Tm, 557th AS Co	18	15
Sup Tm, 2d QM Gp	19	30
Mag Plt, Ammo Co, 57th Ord Gp	30	9.5
TF HQ	151	279
Det, 724th Ord Bn (Abn)	46	54.4
HHC, Log Comd A	69	16
POL Sup Plt (-), 215th QM Bn	54	80
Prov Port Sup Det, 11th Trans Bn	9	1.2
MP Co (-1st Plt), 382d MP Bn	102	21.2
Evac Hosp (Semi-Mbl), 58th Evac Hosp	181	161.3
Sig Spt Co (-), 595th Sig Spt Gp	55	22
Unit Mess Tm, 15th QM Bn	4	4.6
Bath Plt (-), 2d QM Gp	20	10.2
Engr Co (Cbt), Engr Bn	165	236
Trp C (Recon) Abn, 2d Sqd, 9th Cav	157	94
A Btry, 13th FA Bn (Abn)	115	107.7
C Btry, 13th FA Bn (Abn)	115	107.7

	Number	Weight
Prov Arty HQ	39	21.9
D Btry (762 Rkt), 34th FA Bn	56	123.1
Prov Det ASA (USASAE)	64	104
E Co (-) 3d Engr Bn (Abn)	42	165
Det 24th Sig Bn (Abn)	62	24
1st Amb Plt (Abn) 124th Med Bn	28	14.3
Det, 24th Avn Co	62	0
Det, 24th QM Co	39	38
	1,702	1,740.1

APPENDIX D

ON-HAND SUPPLIES, 31 AUGUST 1958

	Beirut	Adana
Class I		
A Rations		
B Rations	200,185	
Cbt Rations	49,005	
Total Tons	249,190	
Days of Sup	29.3	
Classes II and IV		
Total Tons	1,227.2	514
Class III		
AVGAS	18,709 gal	
MOGAS	96,000 gal	
MOGAS (Bulk)	4,773 gal	
Total	119,482 gal	2,106 gal
Days of Sup	26.8	
Class V		
Ordnance	1,102 STON	1,000
Chemical	16.8 STON	
Total Tons	1,118.8	1,000

Total Consumption for August

Water	1,469,296 gal	
MOGAS	199,209 gal	
AVGAS	23,093 gal	

Stored Supplies

Adana

	Stored 1-14 Sep	Total
QM II and IV	2.4	12.5
Ord II and IV	5.2	28.5
Sig II and IV	24.1	33.0
QM III	0	1,775.4
Ord V	2,090.0	2,890
Ord Veh	6.7	136
Cml V	.5	.5
Total Tons	2,138.9	4,875.9

Beirut

On-Hand (14 Sep)

Class I

  B Rations   69,510
  Cbt Rations   47,694
  Five-in-One   1,095

Class II and IV   1,975.3 STON

Class III

  MOGAS   128,440 gal
  AUGAS   63,606 gal

Class V

  Ord   1,034 STON
  Cml   1,683 STON

NOTES

Introduction

1. For further study, see Roger J. Spiller, "Not War But Like War": The American Intervention in Lebanon, Leavenworth Paper no. 3 (Fort Leavenworth, KS: Combat Studies Institute, U.S. Army Command and General Staff College, January 1981).

2. H. H. Lumpkin, "Operation Blue Bat," appendix dated 4 November 1958, to an enclosure, by U.S. European Command dated 17 November 1957, and with subject "Chronology of Operation 'Blue Bat,'" to a Memorandum for the Director, J-2, Joint Chiefs of Staff (Washington, DC, 26 November 1958), 4 (hereafter cited as Lumpkin, "Operation Blue Bat").

3. Press Release no. 280, 6, John Foster Dulles Papers, Princeton University Library, Princeton, NJ.

4. U.S. American Land Forces, Lebanon, "After Action Report, 15 July 58 to 25 October 58, 2d Prov. Marine Force, 24th ABN Brig., 201st Log Cmd," 25 October 1958, 1 (hereafter cited as AMLANFOR, "AAR").

5. "The History of the U.S. Joint Chiefs of Staff," sanitized ed., 442, Records of the Joint Chiefs of Staff, Record Group 218, National Archives, Washington, DC.

6. Lumpkin, "Operation Blue Bat," 4.

7. Support Force Speidel to Commanding General, 24th Infantry Division, 9 August 1958, 4 (hereafter cited as SF Speidel to CG), in U.S. Army, 24th Infantry Division, "After Action Report Operation Grandios, 15-31 July 1958," 5 November 1958 (hereafter cited as 24th ID, "AAR Grandios"). Robert E. Farrell, "Beirut Tests One-Manager Airlift Concept," Aviation Week 69 (11 August 1958):25-27, quotes an unofficial source that set the number of air sorties at 418. This number appears in several later sources. The number 242 denotes the number of aircraft loaded by Support Force Speidel.

8. H. B. Yoshpe and J. Bykofsky, comps., "Lebanon, a Test of Army Contingency Planning," Brief Surveys of the Post-Korean Experience Series (Washington, DC: Chief of Transportation, U.S. Army, 25 November 1958), 21 (hereafter cited as Yoshpe and Bykofsky, "Lebanon").

Chapter 1

1. U.S. Army Command and General Staff College, CGSC 1957-58, "Regular Course Afteraction, Subject nr. 5600-I/8: Introduction to Administrative Support Within Theaters of Operation (Atomic)," pt. 1, "Introduction to Large-Scale Administrative Support," by H. G. Stover, Lt. Col., MPC (Fort Leavenworth, KS, 1 February 1958), 2-1 (hereafter cited as CGSC, "Regular Course").

2. Ibid., 4-1.

3. James A. Huston, The Sinews of War: Army Logistics, 1775-1953, Army Historical Series (Washington, DC: Office of the Chief of Military History, U.S. Army, 1966), 518.

4. CGSC, "Regular Course," 4-1.

5. U.S. Army Service Forces, Logistics in World War II, Final Report of the Army Service Forces, A Report to the Under Secretary of War and the Chief of Staff by the Director of the Service, Supply, and Procurement Division, War Department General Staff, 1 July 1947 (Washington, DC: U.S. Government Printing Office, 1948), 49 (hereafter cited as ASF, Logistics).

6. Huston, Sinews, 557-78.

7. ASF, Logistics, 23-24.

8. Huston, Sinews, 578.

9. CGSC, "Regular Course," 4-1.

10. Ibid., 4-2.

11. U.S. Department of the Army, FM 100-10, Field Service Regulations: Administration, 21 October 1954, 29.

12. Huston, Sinews, 639.

13. Ibid.

14. CGSC, "Regular Course," 4-2.

15. Ibid., 497.

16. Ibid.

17. Ibid., 640.

18. Brig. Gen. (Ret.) Adam W. Meetze to Col. William A. Stofft, 30 July 1982.

19. Yoshpe and Bykofsky, "Lebanon," 3-4.

20. Ibid., 6.

21. Ibid., 8.

22. Ibid., 8 n. 9.

23. Ibid., 8-9.

24. Ibid.

25. Ibid., 10. So as not to "jeopardize higher priority projects," the Air Force, in 1957, canceled production of the new C-132, which was designed to carry 60 tons about 3,500 miles. This action conflicted with the Army's need for newer, heavier, and longer range aircraft. Studies were being conducted, including one for new water-based aircraft, but these were ongoing projects at the time of the Middle East crisis. Yoshpe and Bykofsky, "Lebanon," 10.

26. Farrell, "Beirut Tests," 25.

27. Yoshpe and Bykofsky, "Lebanon," 11.

28. Ibid., 13-14.

29. Ibid., 14.

30. Ibid., 15.

31. U.S. Army, Infantry Conference, Fort Benning, GA, 1958, "Infantry Conference Report 1958: The Lebanon Operation (U)," comments presented by Brig. Gen. David W. Gray, Assistant Division Commander, 24th Infantry Division, 20 February 1959, 211-12 (hereafter cited as "Infantry Conference Report," Comments).

32. Ibid., 212.

33. Ibid.

34. Maj. Gen. (Ret.) David W. Gray, manuscript of his experiences in Lebanon, Combat Studies Institute, U.S. Army Command and General Staff College, Fort Leavenworth, KS, 9.

35. Interview with Brig. Gen. (Ret.) Adam W. Meetze, Princeton, NJ, 12-15 September 1982.

36. U.S. Army, Europe, "Emergency Plan 201," 26 February 1958, (hereafter cited as EP 201).

37. Ibid., sect. IV, 6-7.

38. Yoshpe and Bykofsky, "Lebanon," 17.

39. Ibid.

40. Ibid., 18.

41. EP 201, annex D.

42. Ibid.

43. Yoshpe and Bykofsky, "Lebanon," 24.

44. Col. (Ret.) Dan K. Dukes to Col. William A. Stofft, 9 November 1982.

45. Meetze interview.

46. Meetze to Stofft.

Chapter 2

1. 24th ID, "AAR Grandios," 1.

2. Gray manuscript, 11.

3. Ibid., 9.

4. 24th ID, "AAR Grandios," 12.

5. Gray manuscript, 9.

6. Ibid., 10.

7. Ibid., 16.

8. U.S. Army Task Force 201, Provisional Airborne Brigade, "Command Report for 15-31 July 1958 (U)," Report to Adjutant General, Department of the Army, 13 August 1958, 2 (hereafter cited as PAB, "Command Report").

9. Gray manuscript, 17.

10. SF Speidel to CG, 1.

11. U.S. Army, 11th Airborne Division, "Administrative Plan Grandios," 26 May 1958, 3.

12. AMLANFOR, "AAR," pt. 2, sect. 3, 2.

13. Meetze interview.

14. Gray manuscript, 16.

15. Ibid., 54.

16. U.S. European Command, "Blue Bat Critique, 2-3 December 1958: Final Report on Critique of USCINCEUR participation in CINCSPECOMME OPLAN 215-58," 12 December 1958, 15 (hereafter cited as "Blue Bat Critique").

17. Gray manuscript, 12.

18. Ibid., 18, 9.

19. PAB, "Command Report," 394.

20. Meetze to Stofft.

21. Farrell, "Beirut Tests," 25.

22. Gray manuscript, 24; PAB, "Command Report," 4.

23. Gray manuscript, 24. One airplane was produced in a matter of minutes because it happened to be over Fürstenfeldbruck en route to Évreux when the pilot got the word; the pilot simply lowered the wheels and landed.

24. PAB, "Command Report," 3-4.

25. Gray manuscript, 21-22.

26. Brig. Gen (Ret.) George S. Speidel to Col. William A. Stofft, 20 September 1982.

27. PAB, "Command Report," 4.

28. "Blue Bat Critique," 15.

29. Gray manuscript, 56.

30. Farrell, "Beirut Tests," 26.

31. SF Speidel to CG, 1.

32. Ibid., 4-5.

33. Speidel to Stofft.

34. Gray manuscript, 26.

35. Ibid.

36. SF Speidel to CG, 5.

37. Gray manuscript, 25.

38. PAB, "Command Report," 3.

39. Meetze to Stofft.

40. Yoshpe and Bykofsky, "Lebanon," 20.

41. U.S. Army, 201st Logistical Command, "Historical and Command Report," 15-31 July 1958, 1 (hereafter cited as 201st LC, "Report").

42. Gray manuscript, 32.

43. Ibid., 32-33.

44. Ibid., 34.

45. "Blue Bat Critique," 49.

46. Yoshpe and Bykofsky, "Lebanon," 20.

47. Gray manuscript, 35.

48. "Blue Bat Critique," 18.

49. Ibid., 18.

50. Ibid., 53.

51. Ibid., 21.

52. Yoshpe and Bykofsky, "Lebanon," 21.

53. Ibid.

54. 201st LC, "Report," 15-31 July 1958, 2.

55. Meetze interview.

56. Yoshpe and Bykofsky, "Lebanon," 21.

57. Ibid.

58. U.S. Army, Europe, "Lessons Learned from the Lebanon Operation," Memorandum from the Office of the Chief of Staff to the Deputy Chief of Staff for Military Operations, n.d., tab D, 2.

59. AMLANFOR, "AAR," annex G, sect. 4, pt. 2, subsect. B, 2.

60. "Blue Bat Critique," 45.

61. 201st LC, "Report," 1-31 August 1958, 56.

62. Ibid.

63. Ibid., 55.

64. "Blue Bat Critique," 45.

65. Gray manuscript, 28.

Chapter 3

1. "Blue Bat Critique," 3.

2. Ibid.

3. Ibid.

4. Gray manuscript, 46.

5. "Blue Bat Critique," 3.

6. Ibid.

7. Gray manuscript, 26.

8. Oral history, Gen. (Ret.) Paul D. Adams Papers, U.S. Army Military History Institute, Carlisle Barracks, PA, 24.

9. Gray manuscript, 48.

10. Oral history, Adams Papers, 24-25.

11. U.S. Army, 201st Logistical Command, TFSPO 250/16: "Mission Statement of Headquarters, 201st Logistical Command," 26 September 1958, 1 (hereafter cited as "Mission Statement, 201st Log Comd").

12. Maj. Gen. Paul D. Adams, Commanding Officer, U.S. American Land Forces, Specified Command, Middle East, to

Col. Adam W. Meetze, Commanding Officer, Support Command, "Letter of Instructions," 30 July 1958.

13. "Mission Statement, 201st Log Comd," 1-2.

14. Ibid., 3.

15. Ibid.

16. Dukes to Stofft.

17. Meetze to Stofft.

18. Dukes to Stofft.

19. Ibid.

20. Gray manuscript, 4. In determining class II supplies for individual equipment, General Gray noted that pith helmets were included. General Gray related, "I had participated in a test of this headgear at Ft. Benning in 1934, a test which rejected the helmet as unsuitable for field duty, so I asked that it be stricken from the plan." It was not, but he made "excellent use of about ten of them for the lifeguards on the swimming beach that we established."

21. Yoshpe and Bykofsky, "Lebanon," 22.

22. Meetze to Stofft.

23. Yoshpe and Bykofsky, "Lebanon," 22-23. Concurrent with a reduction in sealift, a CONUS emergency air resupply provided a total of sixty-seven Signal Corps personnel and 164 short tons of Signal Corps, Quartermaster Corps, and Army map service cargo. This suggests planners had ignored these specialists and special technical items or else the men had not been available for deployment with the troops stationed in Europe.

24. Ibid., 23.

25. Meetze to Stofft.

26. AMLANFOR, "AAR," sect. 4, pt. 2, subsect. B, 6-7.

27. 201st LC, "Report," 1-31 August 1958, 25.

28. Ibid., 10, 19-20.

29. U.S. American Land Forces, Lebanon, "Administrative Order 1-58," 31 August 1958, 1 (hereafter cited as AMLANFOR, "AO 1-58").

30. AMLANFOR, "AAR," sect. 4., pt. 2, subsect. B, 5.

31. AMLANFOR, "AAR," sect. 4., pt. 2, annex G, subsect. B, 2.

32. 201st LC, "Report," 1-31 August 1958, 62.

33. AMLANFOR, "AO 1-58," 1.

34. 201st LC, "Report," 1-31 August 1958, 62.

35. "Blue Bat Critique," 37.

36. Ibid.

37. AMLANFOR, "AAR," sect. 4, pt. 2, subsect. B, 6.

38. 201st LC, "Report," 1-31 August 1958, 30.

39. Dukes to Stofft.

40. AMLANFOR, "AAR," sect. 4, pt. 2, annex D, subsect. C, 4.

41. "Blue Bat Critique," 44.

42. U.S. Army, 201st Logistical Command, "Local Procurement of Real Estate, Services and Supply," Staff Study, 12 November 1958, 1 (hereafter cited as 201st LC, "Local Procurement").

43. U. S. Army Communications Zone, Europe, Office of the Director of Procurement, "After Action Report on Procurement, 201st Log Cmd (A)," 16 October 1958, 1 (hereafter cited as ACZE, "AAR").

44. Ibid., comment 1, AEZPD 250/17: "After Action Report, EP 201," 31 October 1958, 1 (hereafter cited as ACZE, "AAR," comment 1).

45. ACZE, "AAR," 1-2.

46. 201st LC, "Report," 15-31 July 1958, 7-8.

47. Ibid., 7. The director of procurement described the procurement practice in a 16 October 1958 report. As definite requirements became known, the contracting officer contacted the appropriate vendors through the embassy. One or more vendors would respond and, after a price was agreed on, the vendor would receive a verbal

order to deliver the required supplies or services. The government thus became obligated through the verbal order of the contracting officer and the subsequent performance of the contractor(s). Occasionally, some typing assistance was available from embassy personnel and, by 31 July 1958, thirteen purchase orders, totaling $5,375.00 had been written. However, the government was also obligated, without benefit of written contract(s), for various supplies; building rentals; petroleum, oils, and lubricants; quarters rental; rail transportation (cargo); and motor transportation (cargo and personnel) and for the cost of unloading ships. As of 31 July, these additional known obligations were estimated to be approximately $30,000. ACZE, "AAR," 1-2.

48. 201st LC, "Local Procurement," 2.

49. Ibid., 1.

50. 201st LC, "Report," 15-31 July 1958, 7.

51. U.S. Army, 201st Logistical Command, "Answers to CONARC and XVIII ABN Questionnaire," 6 October 1958, 2.

52. ACZE, "AAR," comment 1, 2.

53. Gray manuscript, 3.

54. Meetze to Stofft.

55. U.S. Department of Defense, Office of Civil Affairs Military Group, Plans, Policy, and Operations Division, "Civil Affairs in the Lebanon Operation," 19 January 1959, 7-8 (hereafter cited as DOD, "Civil Affairs").

56. Meetze to Stofft; DOD, "Civil Affairs," 7-8.

57. DOD, "Civil Affairs," 3.

58. Ibid.

59. "Blue Bat Critique," 28-30.

60. DOD, "Civil Affairs," 4.

61. Ibid., 5.

62. Ibid.

63. "Blue Bat Critique," 29.

64. Ibid.

65. DOD, "Civil Affairs," 9.

66. Ibid., 9-10.

67. Ibid., 10-11.

68. Ibid., 13.

69. Ibid.

70. Ibid., 14.

71. Col. (Ret.) Richard M. Hermann to Col. William A. Stofft, 25 August 1982.

72. U.S. Department of Defense, Assistant Secretary (Health and Medical), "Evaluation of Medical Service Support for the Lebanon Operation," 18 February 1960, 15 (hereafter cited as DOD, "Evaluation").

73. Ibid., 3.

74. Ibid.

75. Ibid., 14.

76. Ibid.

77. Ibid., 13.

78. Ibid., 14.

79. "Blue Bat Critique," 37.

80. DOD, "Evaluation," 7-8.

81. 201st LC, "Report," 1-31 August 1958, 40.

82. Ibid.

83. DOD, "Evaluation," 12.

84. Gray manuscript, 3.

85. Ibid.

86. "Infantry Conference Report," Comments, 228.

87. Ibid.

88. Ibid.

89. 201st LC, "Report," 1-31 August 1958, 24.

90. 201st LC, "Report," 15-31 July 1958, 3.

91. 201st LC, "Report," 1-31 August 1958, 7.

92. Meetze to Stofft.

Chapter 4

1. 201st LC, "Report," 13 October-30 November 1958, 1.

2. U.S. Army, Europe, General Order 348, 10 November 1958.

GLOSSARY

AMLANFOR: American Land Forces.

ATF 201: Army Task Force 201.

Automatic requisitions: Equipment, materiel, repair parts, and resupply necessary to support an operation in the planning phase and would on a predetermined time schedule be sent to a using unit. Automatic requisitions are used to maintain a specific stockage level in the forward areas.

BG: Battle Group.

CALSU: Combat air logistic support unit.

CINC: Commander in Chief.

CINCNELM: Commander in Chief, Naval Element, Mediterranean.

CINCSPECOMME: Commander in Chief, Specified Command, Middle East.

CINCUSAFE: Commander in Chief, U.S. Air Force, Europe.

COMAIRSPECOMME: Commander, U.S. Air Forces, Specified Command, Middle East.

COMAMLANFOR: Commander, American Land Forces.

Combat loaded: A method of loading essential equipment and supplies so that they can be unloaded ready for action.

Combat service support: Services provided to combat troops, such as maintenance of equipment, repair parts, quartermaster resupply, laundry services, ammunition resupply, etc.

Communications Zone (COMMZ): The region that connects the part of an army actually fighting with its sources of supply. It is a part of the theater of operations behind the combat zone. Within this zone are supply and evacuation establishments, repair shops, and other service facilities.

CONUS: Continental United States.

CPX: Command post exercise.

CRAF: Civil Reserve Air Fleet.

DA: Department of the Army.

DCSLOG: Deputy Chief of Staff for Logistics.

DOD: Department of Defense.

E-day: The day plans became orders.

EP 201: Emergency Plan 201.

EUCOM: European Command.

Indigenous labor: Native people hired for various tasks in support of a military operation.

JCS: Joint Chiefs of Staff.

Logistics: Art of planning and carrying out military movement, evacuation, and supply.

MATS: Military Air Transportation Service.

Measurement ton: Measure of cubic volume of cargo, expressed in units of 40 cubic feet. It is also used to indicate the cubic capacity of a ship's available cargo space.

MSTS: Military Sea Transporation Service.

OPLAN: Operations plan.

Organic support troops: Personnel assigned to a combat unit whose duties are to provide the internal combat service support for that unit.

Pentomic: A divisional organization consisting of five battle groups, each a self-contained force capable of independent operations. This organization was to provide the mobile units necessary for nuclear war.

Precut requisitions: The system of filing requisition forms in support of automatic resupply.

Pull system: A system whereby a unit asked, by means of a requistion, for materiel that was then acquired by the support unit and sent to the asking unit.

Push-pull system: A system whereby a unit predetermines its own needs for an upcoming operation. The materiel is then packaged in sets of determined quantity, and, after the unit is deployed, it requests by requisition a specific number of these sets as needed. The support unit then sends the required number of sets.

Push system: A system whereby automatic requisitioned materiel is sent by support units to using units on a predetermined time schedule.

ROCID: Reorganization of Current Infantry Divisions.

Roll-on/Roll-off ship: A ship in which vehicles can drive on and drive off under their own power.

ROTAD: Reorganization of the Airborne Division.

Sea tail: That part of an airborne or air-transported unit that is not committed to combat by air and will join the organization by sea travel.

SETAF: Southern European Task Force.

Short ton: 2,000 pounds or 0.907 metric tons. Often used in place of long ton (2,240 pounds) to simplify calculations.

SPECOMME: Specified Command, Middle East.

STRAC: Strategic Army Corps.

Supported forces: Forces receiving support either from combat units or combat service support units.

Supporting forces: Forces providing the support to the supported forces and not under the command of the supported forces.

Technical service: One of the branches of the Army, such the Quartermaster Corps or the Ordnance Department, whose chief mission was the procurement and distribution of supplies needed by various units of the Army.

TOE: Table of organization and equipment.

Ton miles: The lift capacity to carry 2,000 pounds one mile. It would take one million ton miles to carry 1,000 tons 1,000 miles.

Unit requisitions: A method of filing requisitions in support of a pull system.

USAREUR: U.S. Army, Europe.

BIBLIOGRAPHY

Adams, Paul D., Maj. Gen., Commanding Officer, U.S. American Land Forces, Specified Command, Middle East, to Col. Adam W. Meetze, Commanding Officer, Support Command. "Letter of Instructions." 30 July 1958.

_____, Gen. (Ret.). Papers. U.S. Army Military History Institute, Carlisle Barracks, PA.

Clarke, Philip C. "Rapid Deployment Force: How Real a Deterrent?" The American Legion Magazine 110 (June 1981):18-19, 37-39.

Collins, John M., and Clyde R. Mark. "Petroleum Imports from the Persian Gulf: Use of U.S. Armed Forces to Ensure Supplies." Library of Congress Congressional Research Service, Major Issues System, Issue Brief no. 1B 79046. Washington, DC: Library of Congress, 26 April 1979, updated 4 January 1982.

DiLeonardo, Anthony D. "The Persian Gulf: Can the United States Defend the Flow of Oil?" Master of Military Art and Science thesis, U.S. Army Command and General Staff College, Fort Leavenworth, KS, 1981.

Dukes, Dan K., Col. (Ret.). Letter to Col. William A. Stofft, 9 November 1982.

Dulles, John Foster. Papers. Princeton University Library, Princeton, NJ.

Farrell, Robert E. "Beirut Tests One-Manager Airlift Concept." Aviation Week 69 (11 August 1958):25-27.

Gordon, Michael R. "The Rapid Deployment Force--Too Large, Too Small, or Just Right." National Journal 14 (13 March 1982):451-55.

Gray, David M., Maj. Gen. (Ret.). Manuscript of his experiences in Lebanon. Combat Studies Institute, U.S. Army Command and General Staff College, Fort Leavenworth, KS.

Hadd, H. A. "Orders Firm But Flexible." U.S. Naval Institute Proceedings 88 (October 1962):81-89.

Hermann, Richard M., Col. (Ret.). Letter to Col. William A. Stofft, 25 August 1982.

"The History of the Joint Chiefs of Staff." Sanitized ed. Records of the U.S. Joint Chiefs of Staff. Record Group 218. National Archives, Washington, DC.

Huston, James A. The Sinews of War: Army Logistics, 1775-1953. Army Historical Series. Washington, DC: Office of the Chief of Military History, U.S. Army, 1966.

Jane's All the World's Aircraft, 1957-1958. New York: McGraw-Hill Book Co., 1957.

Jane's Fighting Ships, 1957-1958. New York: McGraw-Hill Book Co., 1957.

Lumpkin, H. H. "Operation Blue Bat." Appendix dated 4 November 1958 to an enclosure, by U.S. European Command dated 17 November 1957 and with subject "Chronology of Operation 'Blue Bat,'" to a Memorandum for the Director, J-2, Joint Chiefs of Staff. Washington, DC, 26 November 1958.

McClintock, Robert. "The American Landing in Lebanon." U.S. Naval Institute Proceedings 88 (October 1962): 65-79.

Meetze, Adam W., Brig. Gen. (Ret.). Interview with author. Princeton, NJ, 12-15 September 1982.

_____. Letter to Col. William A. Stofft, 30 July 1982.

_____. Papers Dealing with the Lebanon Intervention. Combat Studies Institute, U.S. Army Command and General Staff College, Fort Leavenworth, KS.

Meloy, Guy S. "A Look Back at Lebanon." Infantry 50 (January 1960):22-25.

Nielsen, John, et al. "The Carter Doctrine: Can We Defend the Gulf?" Newsweek, 4 February 1980:25-26.

Qubain, Fahim I. Crisis in Lebanon. Washington, DC: Middle East Institute, 1961.

"Rapid Deployment Task Force to Become Separate Command." Aviation Week & Space Technology 114 (11 May 1981):77.

Record, Jeffrey. "Rapid Deployment Force: Problems, Constraints, and Needs." Annals of the American Academy of Political and Social Science 457 (September 1981):109-20.

Speidel, George S., Brig. Gen. (Ret.). Letter to Col. William A. Stofft, 20 September 1982.

Spiller, Roger J. "Not War But Like War": The American Intervention in Lebanon. Leavenworth Paper no. 3. Fort Leavenworth, KS: Combat Studies Institute, U.S. Army Command and General Staff College, January 1981.

Taylor, Maxwell D. The Uncertain Trumpet. New York: Harper & Brothers, 1959.

U.S. American Land Forces, Lebanon. "Administrative Order 1-58." 31 August 1958.

_____. "After Action Report, 15 July 58 to 25 October 58, 2d Prov. Marine Force, 24th ABN Brig., 201st Log Comd." 25 October 1958.

_____. Lebanon Crisis 1958. 6 boxes. Record Group 338. National Archives, Washington, DC.

U.S. Army. 11th Airborne Division. "Administrative Plan Grandios." 26 May 1958.

U.S. Army Command and General Staff College. CGSC 1957-58. "Regular Course Afteraction, Subject nr. 5600-1/8: Introduction to Administrative Support Within Theaters of Operation (Atomic)." Pt. 1. "Introduction to Large-Scale Administrative Support." By H. G. Stover, Lt. Col., MPC. Fort Leavenworth, KS, 1 February 1958.

U.S. Army Communications Zone, Europe. Office of the Director of Procurement. "After Action Report on Procurement, 201st Log. Cmd (A)." 16 October 1958. With Comment 1 AEZPD 250/17: "After Action Report, EP201." 31 October 1958.

U.S. Army, Europe. "Emergency Plan 201." 26 February 1958.

_____. General Order 348. 10 November 1958.

_____. "Lessons Learned from the Lebanon Operation." Memorandum from the Office of the Chief of Staff to the Deputy Chief of Staff for Military Operations. n.d.

U.S. Army. Infantry Conference, Fort Benning, GA, 1958. "Infantry Conference Report 1958: The Lebanon Operation. (U)." Comments presented by Brig. Gen. David W. Gray, Assistant Division Commander, 24th Infantry Division, 20 February 1959. Pages 210-29 declassified.

U.S. Army. 24th Infantry Division. "After Action Report Operation Grandios, 15-31 July 1958. 5 November 1958. With enclosure, "Operation Plan GRANDIOS," 1 July 1958.

U.S. Army. 201st Logistical Command. "Answers to CONARC and XVIII ABN Questionnaire." 6 October 1958.

_____. "Historical and Command Reports, 15 July to 30 November 1958, of 201st Log. Command." Including "Letter of Instruction, 30 July 1958.

_____. "Local Procurement of Real Estate, Services, and Supplies." Staff Study. 12 November 1958.

_____. TFSPO 250/16: "Mission Statement of Headquarters, 201st Logistical Command." 26 September 1958.

U.S. Army Service Forces. <u>Logistics in World War II, Final Report of the Army Service Forces</u>. A Report to the Under Secretary of War and the Chief of Staff by the Director of the Service, Supply, and Procurement Division, War Department General Staff, 1 July 1947. Washington, DC: U.S. Government Printing Office, 1948.

U.S. Army. Task Force 201. Provisional Airborne Brigade. "Command Report for 15-31 July 1958. (U)" Report to Adjutant General, Department of the Army. 13 August 1958.

U.S. Department of Defense. Assistant Secretary (Health and Medical). "Evaluation of Medical Service Support for the Lebanon Operation." 18 February 1960.

U.S. Department of Defense. Office of Civil Affairs Military Group. Plans, Policy, and Operations Division. "Civil Affairs in the Lebanon Operation." 19 January 1959.

U.S. Department of the Army. FM 54-1. <u>The Logistical Command</u>. July 1959.

_____. FM 100-5. <u>Field Service Regulations: Operations</u>. September 1954.

_____. FM 100-10. <u>Field Service Regulations: Adminstration</u>. 21 October 1954. With changes 1-3.

_____. "Lessons Learned from Lebanon Operation." Memorandum from the Deputy Chief of Staff for Military Operations to the Chief of Staff, U.S. Army, n.d.

U.S. European Command. "Blue Bat Critique, 2-3 December 1958: Final Report on Critique of USCINCEUR Participation in CINCSPECOMME OPLAN 215-58." 12 December 1958.

Weigley, Russell Frank. *The American Way of War: A History of United States Military Strategy and Policy*. New York: Macmillan Co., 1973.

Yoshpe, H. B., and J. Bykofsky, comps. "Lebanon, a Test of Army Contingency Planning." Brief Surveys of the Post-Korean Experience Series. Washington, DC: Chief of Transportation, U.S. Army, 25 November 1958.

www.ingramcontent.com/pod-product-compliance
Lightning Source LLC
Chambersburg PA
CBHW082235170426
43196CB00041B/2790